Andronik, Catherine M.
Stephen Colbert

STEPHEN COLBERT

Recent Titles in Greenwood Biographies

STEPHEN COLBERT

A Biography

Catherine M. Andronik

GREENWOOD BIOGRAPHIES

 GREENWOOD

AN IMPRINT OF ABC-CLIO, LLC
Santa Barbara, California • Denver, Colorado • Oxford, England

Copyright 2012 by ABC-CLIO, LLC

All rights reserved. No part of this publication may be reproduced,
stored in a retrieval system, or transmitted, in any form or by any means,
electronic, mechanical, photocopying, recording, or otherwise, except
for the inclusion of brief quotations in a review, without prior permission
in writing from the publisher.

Library of Congress Cataloging-in-Publication Data

Andronik, Catherine M.
  Stephen Colbert : a biography / Catherine M. Andronik.
     p. cm. — (Greenwood biographies)
  Includes bibliographical references and index.
  ISBN 978-0-313-38628-2 (hardcopy : alk. paper) — ISBN 978-0-313-38629-9
(ebook) 1. Colbert, Stephen, 1964– 2. Television personalities—United
States—Biography. 3. Comedians—United States—Biography. I. Title.
  PN2287.C5695A58   2012
  792.702'8092—dc23
  [B]   2011053334

ISBN: 978-0-313-38628-2
EISBN: 978-0-313-38629-9

16 15 14 13 12   1 2 3 4 5

This book is also available on the World Wide Web as an eBook.
Visit www.abc-clio.com for details.

Greenwood
An Imprint of ABC-CLIO, LLC

ABC-CLIO, LLC
130 Cremona Drive, P.O. Box 1911
Santa Barbara, California 93116-1911

This book is printed on acid-free paper ∞

Manufactured in the United States of America

CONTENTS

SERIES FOREWORD

In response to school and library needs, ABC-CLIO publishes this distinguished series of full-length biographies specifically for student use. Prepared by field experts and professionals, these engaging biographies are tailored for students who need challenging yet accessible biographies. Ideal for school assignments and student research, the length, format, and subject areas are designed to meet educators' requirements and students' interests.

ABC-CLIO offers an extensive selection of biographies spanning all curriculum-related subject areas including social studies, the sciences, literature and the arts, history and politics, and popular culture, covering public figures and famous personalities from all time periods and backgrounds, both historic and contemporary, who have made an impact on American and/or world culture. The subjects of these biographies were chosen based on comprehensive feedback from librarians and educators. Consideration was given to both curriculum relevance and inherent interest. Readers will find a wide array of subject choices from fascinating entertainers like Miley Cyrus and Lady Gaga to inspiring leaders like John F. Kennedy and Nelson Mandela, from the greatest athletes of our time like Michael Jordan and Lance Armstrong to the most amazing success stories of our day like J.K. Rowling and Oprah.

While the emphasis is on fact, not glorification, the books are meant to be fun to read. Each volume provides in-depth information about the subject's life from birth through childhood, the teen years, and adulthood. A thorough account relates family background and education, traces personal and professional influences, and explores struggles, accomplishments, and contributions. A timeline highlights the most significant life events against an historical perspective. Bibliographies supplement the reference value of each volume.

INTRODUCTION

Stephen Tyrone Colbert is an American comedian and actor who has built a following around the character he created—a character who is also named Stephen Colbert. Since 2005, he has hosted an Emmy-winning television show, *The Colbert Report,* on the cable channel Comedy Central. Colbert's character is a satirical version of conservative political pundits like Bill O'Reilly. Colbert the real person claims two honorary doctorates and Jordanian knighthood, and he sometimes does add the titles Dr. and Dr., Sir to his name, though usually as a joke.

Colbert was born on May 13, 1964, the 11th and last child in his family. He grew up in Charleston, South Carolina. When he was 10 years old, his father and two brothers were killed in a plane crash as they were traveling to Connecticut to drop off the boys at boarding school. As all the other siblings were older, Stephen lived alone with his mother until he went away to college. Although the Colbert family is Catholic, Stephen attended Porter-Gaud School, a private Episcopal high school in Charleston. While in his teens, he became interested in drama and theater. For two years he attended Sydney-Hampden College in Virginia, an all-male institution, where he studied philosophy. Unhappy there, he transferred to Northwestern University in Evanston, Illinois, as a communications/theater major. Though his intent was to become a serious dramatic actor, friends drew him into Chicago's rich world of improvisational theater. After graduation from Northwestern in 1986, he joined Second City, the premier American training ground for improvisational comedians. With Second City, he was in a traveling company with the late Chris Farley (of *Saturday Night Live*), Amy Sedaris, and Paul Dinello and served as understudy for future coworker Steve Carell.

Colbert found kindred spirits in Sedaris and Dinello. The three moved to New York, where they wrote and acted in several short-lived series for Comedy Central. *Exit 57* looked at the weird and wacky lives of a group of young people. *Strangers with Candy*, their most successful endeavor, was about a problem teen who returns to high school decades later to get her diploma and is now a problem adult; it spawned a movie of the same title. If one watches the credits for *Strangers with Candy*, one might notice a certain Evelyn McGee—aka Mrs. Stephen Colbert. McGee was also a Charleston native; the two met in 1990, married, and have raised a family of three very non-show-business children. Colbert was also involved in writing for the short-lived *The Dana Carvey Show*.

Among Comedy Central's programs in the late 1990s was *The Daily Show*, hosted at first by Craig Kilborn. The program was a send-up of real newscasts, complete with a team of correspondents. For a short time in the Kilborn years, those correspondents included Colbert. He also tried his hand at real news for ABC's *Good Morning, America*, where he covered humorous human interest stories. Only one of his pieces actually aired.

In 1999, Craig Kilborn left *The Daily Show* and was replaced by Jon Stewart, an actor and stand-up comedian who had previously hosted a talk show on MTV. Reluctantly, Colbert accepted an offer to rejoin the cast of *The Daily Show*. With the smart, biting wit of Stewart at the helm, the show skyrocketed to success. Colbert began developing his character, a "poorly informed, high-status idiot," as a foil to Stewart. As many of *The Daily Show*'s other correspondents—Steve Carell, Ed Helms, Rob Corddry—left the show for other movie or television projects, Comedy Central looked for a way to keep Colbert in its stable. What developed was a *Daily Show* spinoff, *The Colbert Report*.

The Colbert Report parodies the shows of such pundits as Bill O'Reilly and Rush Limbaugh. Colbert proclaims his conservative version of the truth loudly and bombastically and refuses to be swayed from his beliefs by mere facts. His guests on the show have run the gamut from politicians to scientists to rock bands, from the sublime to the ridiculous. None are spared from Colbert's sharp tongue. The show engendered a fan following, known as Colbert Nation, which wields considerable clout in the real world.

The real Stephen Colbert should not be mistaken for the character of the same name; while there is some overlap between the two, they are not the same. Both are proud, vocal Catholics; the real Stephen Colbert actually teaches Sunday school without his trademark irony. Whereas the character is staunchly Republican, the real Stephen Colbert holds a more Democratic views. And sometimes it is difficult to say whether an accomplishment belongs to the man or the character. Queen Noor of Jordan, for instance, knighted Stephen on one episode of his show—but, since he was in character, is *he* entitled to be called Sir, or just his character? He holds two honorary doctorates of fine arts, one from Knox College, the other from his alma mater, Northwestern University. Colbert lives with his wife and three children in New Jersey, a short commute to the Manhattan studio where *The Colbert Report* is taped.

TIMELINE: EVENTS IN THE LIFE OF STEPHEN COLBERT

May 13, 1964	Stephen Tyrone Colbert is born.
September 11, 1974	Stephen's father, Dr. James Colbert, and brothers, Paul and Peter, are killed in a plane crash.
1986	Graduates from Northwestern University.
Early 1990s	Joins Second City.
1995–1996	With Amy Sedaris and Paul Dinello, creates *Exit 57* for Comedy Central.
1997	Joins cast of *The Daily Show* with Craig Kilborn.
1997	Correspondent for *Good Morning, America*.
1998–2000	With Amy Sedaris and Paul Dinello, creates *Strangers with Candy* for Comedy Central.
1999	Rejoins cast of *The Daily Show* with Jon Stewart.
2000	Presidential election coverage for *The Daily Show*.
2003	Publication of *Wigfield*.
2004	Presidential election coverage for *The Daily Show*.
October 17, 2005	Launch of *The Colbert Report* on Comedy Central.

April 29, 2006	Comedy guest at White House Correspondents' Dinner.
2007	Publication of *I Am America (And So Can You!)*.
October 16, 2007	Declares presidential candidacy in South Carolina.
November 5, 2007	Drops presidential bid.
November 5, 2007	Writers Guild of America strike begins.
February 12, 2008	Writers Guild of America strike ends.
November 23, 2008	*A Colbert Christmas* airs.
June 8–11, 2009	Operation Iraqi Stephen airs.
September 24, 2010	Testifies before Congress on immigration.
October 30, 2010	Rally to Restore Sanity and/or Fear, Washington, D.C.
April 7–9, 2011	Sondheim's *Company* with New York Philharmonic.
June 30, 2011	SuperPac approved.

Chapter 1

STUDIO AUDIENCE

The line snakes up and down a covered alleyway on 54th Street in Manhattan, between 10th and 11th Avenues. It is about 5:30 P.M.; some of these people have already been here for quite a while. There are about as many men as women; most appear to be in their mid-20s, though quite a few others could be called mature adults. Their goal: entrance into the building that abuts the alley, the building with a red, white, and blue marqueed awning designating the studio where *The Colbert Report* is taped at about 7:30, Monday through Thursday evenings, 161 days a year, in front of a studio audience. About 120 of these people will be the lucky ones who reach that goal. Most clutch email printouts confirming that they requested tickets online. Others are hoping that it is a slow day for confirmed ticketholders and they will gain entrance as stand-bys. On the alley wall, a sketch of Stephen Colbert, eyebrow cocked, asks the waiting throngs to please refrain from defacing the building with graffiti. The wall is, as requested, graffiti-free.

Before long, staffers with clipboards and stacks of blue laminated tickets bearing Colbert's cartoon likeness and a number make their way through the line, checking names against the email records. "Are you ready to laugh tonight?" they ask energetically. There are also tickets on red or white paper, which designate preferred seating. Among those tapped for these front-row seats are members of the armed services— and extreme early birds. Patience and determination pay off.

The line gradually shuffles forward, and finally, with enough people to fill each and every seat in the studio, that evening's audience is assembled to mill about in a chairless waiting room. Tickets to the taping are limited, but free; those left out in the alley will probably try another day—and arrive earlier.

Inside the tiny waiting room, a large-screen television on one wall streams the DVD *The Best of the Colbert Report*, featuring clips from some of Colbert's shows from 2005 to 2007. Meanwhile, another staffer explains the studio protocol: turn off your cell phones, no cameras or other recording devices, no food or drink during the taping.

Finally, the studio doors open and the audience files in to take its seats. It is semicircular amphitheater-style seating, a good view from everywhere, not a bad spot in the house. Monitors are set up so the audience can see what viewers at home will see, such as the graphics frequently used in *The Colbert Report* sketches. The live set—which Colbert and his staff refer to as the "Eagle's Nest"[1]—seems smaller than it looks on television, but everything is there: the omnipresent blazing red, white, and blue graphics; the wraparound desk with its comfy-looking, ergonomic office chair; the bookshelves crammed with items memorializing the host and his accomplishments—from a model racing yacht to a Rock 'em-Sock 'em Robot game; the round polished wood table in front of a cozy electric fireplace where Colbert interviews each evening's special guests. The trademark capital C is everywhere. Colbert has said that the design of the Eagle's Nest recalls, in a weird way, Leonardo da Vinci's painting *The Last Supper*. He actually instructed his set designer to study the painting. "All the architecture of that room points at Jesus's head, the entire room is a halo, and he doesn't have a halo. On the set, I'd like the lines of the set to converge on my head. And so if you look at the design, it all does, it all points at my head. And even radial lines on the floor, and on my podium, and watermarks in the images behind me, and all the vertices, are right behind my head. So there's a sort of sun-god burst quality about the set around me."[2] The meticulous design of the set also has to do with Colbert's vision of his character as *not* a newscaster, but as news himself. "I said [to the designer], 'I am the news. I translate nothing. I am not a medium. I am not a member of the media, because I'm not a vessel. I am it.'"[3]

The theme music for *The Colbert Report* was just as carefully planned as the layout of the studio. Titled "Baby Muggles," it's by the 1970s rock band Cheap Trick, best known for hits like "The Flame" and "Surrender."[4] When the band was composing it, Colbert suggested it take Aaron Copland's "Fanfare for the Common Man" as inspiration for grandeur. "If you can put majesty on top, with something that rocks for 15 seconds, and with a discernible melody, that'd be great."[5]

But we haven't gotten to "Baby Muggles" yet. Instead, music with a strong dance beat blasts from studio's speakers, adding to the feeling that you've just crashed a very cool party.

The stage manager comes out to explain the audience's crucial role in the evening's show. Colbert, he explains, was trained in improvisational comedy. An enthusiastic, laughing, engaged audience encourages improvisational or stand-up comedians to ad-lib, to deviate a bit from the prepared script; a good audience really can make the show funnier. He demonstrates the signal for a strong audience response, which could include standing, cheering, clapping, woo-hooing, chanting. This behavior is appropriate for the beginning of the show and returns from commercial breaks. It is, however, not appropriate during Colbert's commentary, when anything from chuckles to hearty laughs are all that are required. And, the stage manager assures us, this is Stephen Colbert. Laughing will not be a chore; it should come quite easily.

Production-wise, about 90 people make each night's *The Colbert Report* happen. Some the audience gets to see—the crew making its way around the stage, checking lights, cameras, microphones, and monitors. Others work behind the scenes. For instance, Colbert does not write his scripts alone; he collaborates with a team of a dozen talented writers. At a little past 7:00 P.M., a staffer enters from the wings with sheaves of paper in his hands. Carefully, neatly, he places one stack on the C-shaped desk at center stage. "Okay, we've got a script," he can be heard to say quietly.[6] The behind-the-scenes work is done for the day. Besides Colbert's script on the desk, a copy is also transcribed into a teleprompter so Colbert can read it while apparently looking at the camera.

Soon after, a stand-up comedian enters to warm up the audience. He singles out one or two people and asks questions, then bases his act on their responses. It gets people laughing freely, primed for more. At last, he introduces the star of the show, and Colbert himself skips onstage from behind his desk.

For just these few minutes before the actual show, the studio audience is allowed to see the *real* Colbert, the man, not the character he has created. He calls this his opportunity to humanize himself. People in the audience volunteer questions, and, out of character, Colbert answers them. That evening, subjects range from the college commencement addresses he gave recently, to his favorite Harry Potter character, Professor Lupin. ("I love those books. But poor Tonks," Colbert adds.) There is also an unexpectedly, somewhat embarrassingly funny exchange based on the phrase "Who's the Man?" A reference to the flub reappears as an ad-lib a few minutes later in the show itself. With a professional's full control of his audience, Colbert suddenly calls an end to the question-and-answer session—no one clamors for just one more comment. He takes a seat at his desk for a quick makeup touch-up. A spritz of hairspray on his signature brunette forelock gets the audience cheering. Afterward he playfully shoots a few rubber bands into the audience, looks about for something else to throw, and, finally, with a wicked grin, produces an equally wicked-looking knife from under the desk. There are no takers. Then he disappears backstage once again.[7]

The next time the audience sees Colbert, it is on its feet, cheering, as he lopes in from the wings of the stage just as on television, looking, between his conservative dark suit and his huge grin, "like a gleeful bank manager who's just won the lottery or possibly lost his mind."[8] He tosses his microphone high in the air like a cheerleader's baton, encourages the cheers, and the audience plays along, finally breaking into a rhythmic chant of "Stee-phen, Stee-phen, Stee-phen!" before calming down for the show to begin.

Tapings of some television shows can be deadly boring. There are takes and retakes, flubbed lines, messy camera angles. A half hour program can take over an hour to record. *The Colbert Report* is not one of those shows. What is seen on television is essentially identical to what the studio audience sees. There is not a lot of time for editing afterward; each night's live show must be ready for its television airing at 11:30 P.M. That evening, as Colbert finishes one particularly long, breathlessly rapid-fire monologue, he begins to crack up on camera. "That's a lot of words!" he says, recovering. As the crew looks through the tape to the point where he would like to start a second take, seated behind his desk Colbert mimics the sound of a tape recorder in rapid rewind. On the retake he also tweaks the segment's final joke. It is much funnier the second time through.[9]

Commercial breaks are busy times on the set. Writers huddle with Colbert, shuffling the papers of the script, pointing and whispering. Staffers escort guests to their seats and make them comfortable. Not a moment is wasted on this soundstage. At times like these, the studio audience sits forgotten. But at any time when Colbert the character is "on," he occasionally tosses his audience a glance, a wink, a grin, a classic raised eyebrow. He is playing to them, and they are definitely *not* forgotten.

After all, it's his fans—aka Colbert Nation—who have gotten Colbert to where he is today.

NOTES

1. "The Eagle's Nest." *Wikiality, the Truthiness Encyclopedia.* Web. 31 July 2011. <http://wikiality.wikia.com/The_Eagle's_Nest>.

2. Rabin, Nathan. "Interview with Stephen Colbert from The Onion's AV Club." *Enter Tony's "Strangers with Candy Companion."* 26 Jan. 2006. Web. 31 July 2011. <http://www.jerriblank.com/colbert_onion-av-club.html>.

3. Strauss, Neil. "The Subversive Joy of Stephen Colbert. (cover story)." *Rolling Stone* 1087 (2009): 56. MAS Ultra—School Edition. EBSCO. Web. 13 Oct. 2011.

4. "'The Colbert Report' (2005)—Soundtracks." *The Internet Movie Database (IMDb).* Web. 08 Aug. 2011. <http://www.imdb.com/title/tt0458254/soundtrack>.

5. Edwards, Gavin. "Colbert Country." *Rolling Stone* 986 (2005): 68. MAS Ultra—School Edition. EBSCO. Web. 16 Oct. 2011.

6. *The Colbert Report.* New York. 13 July 2011. Performance.

7. *The Colbert Report.* New York. 13 July 2011.

8. Sternbergh, Adam. "Stephen Colbert has America by the ballots: The former Jon Stewart protégé created an entire comic persona out of right-wing doublespeak, trampling the boundary between parody and politics. Which makes him the perfect spokesman for a political season in which everything is imploding." *New York* 16 Oct. 2006: 22+. *General OneFile*. Web. 23 July 2010.

9. *The Colbert Report*. New York. 13 July 2011.

Chapter 2

BABY OF THE FAMILY

On May 13, 1964, the Colbert family of Charleston, South Carolina, welcomed baby Stephen Tyrone into the world. It may have been a portent of his future as a comedian with one finger on the pulse of the political scene that he was born, not in Charleston, but in Washington, D.C. Stephen's father, James, trained as an immunologist, was also vice president for academic affairs at the Medical University of South Carolina. His mother, Lorna, was a stay-at-home mom. The Colberts already had a big family of 10 children: Jimmy, Eddie, Mary, Billy, Margot, Tommy, Jay, Lulu, Paul, and Peter. Stephen, number 11, would be their final child. The family lived just across the harbor from Charleston proper, on James Island. The island is the site of Fort Johnson, where the first Confederate shots were fired on nearby Union-occupied Fort Sumter, marking the opening engagement of the Civil War. There is actually a section of the community that is called Secessionville.

Growing up on pleasant, suburban James Island, Colbert enjoyed the busy, bustling household that comes with being part of a large, unabashedly affectionate family in which he was known as The Prince. His sister Lulu compares having a baby Stephen in the house to getting a new doll.[1] Colbert agrees. "I was very loved. My sisters like to say that they are surprised that I learned to walk and that my legs didn't become vestigial because I got carried around by them so much."[2] It would be easy for a child's personality to be lost among 12 other people, but Colbert had a special talent: he could make the people around him, especially his mother, laugh. He also thought he was good at making up stories, though his sisters and brothers would have disagreed. "You listen to his stories!" Lorna would admonish her older children. Dutifully, they humored their youngest brother.[3] But in no way was Stephen the only talented member of the Colbert clan. While he definitely had competition when it came to storytelling, he found himself envying his older siblings for many things—their senses of humor, their glorious singing voices. "I think my brothers and sisters are way funnier than I am—and they think they're funnier than I am, too. Ask them, and they'll tell you. I wanted to tell stories like Ed, tell jokes like Billy, have a rapier wit like Jim, be quick like Mary, or sing like Margot."[4]

The Colberts were, and are, a staunchly Irish American Catholic family, going to Mass every Sunday and observing religious rituals like Lent and confession. Colbert's first stage experience came early. While in kindergarten, he was in a Christmas pageant. And leave it to him to rewrite the Bible: he played a *fourth* Wise Man.[5] When he was seven years old, he became an altar boy at the family's parish church. He continued to serve at Masses, weddings, and funerals for the next 11 years, until he went away to college. In some ways Colbert regretted missing out on the altar boy experience his older brothers had had, pre-Vatican II. When it was his time to serve, the parish had switched from traditional Latin to a guitar-playing folk Mass. "I really wanted to wear the black cassock with the white surplice over it because . . . you look like a mini-priest when you've got the cassock on," he recalls. Instead, as an altar boy he wore a sort of monk's robe, complete with rope belt.[6]

His early upbringing also set the stage for the way Colbert now questions truth and authority. "I grew up in a family that valued intelligence," he says.[7] For some fiercely religious people, doubts are a sign that you don't truly believe. For the Colberts, doubting and inquiry were encouraged. Dr. Colbert raised his children to believe that asking questions, even about matters that are supposed to be accepted without question—like religion—is the only way to really understand your beliefs. Stephen and his siblings grew up aware that skepticism can be a healthy thing.

While he was still young, his parents discovered that Colbert had difficulty hearing out of his right ear. Depending on what source one believes, the problem was either a tumor (removed "with a melon baller," adult Colbert has quipped)[8] or complications from surgery for a perforated eardrum. Whatever the true cause, Colbert has no eardrum in his right ear and continues to be deaf on that side. The handicap has not affected his career. In fact, if he wants to he can turn his bad ear into a potential comic prop: he claims that he is able to twist that ear inside out, then pop it back into shape with a squint of his eye.[9] The lack of an eardrum did, however, prevent him from participating in water sports as a child. He longed to learn to sail in a waterfront town renowned for its regattas and races. When he was 20 and fully healed, his mother did offer to pay for sailing lessons, but he did not actually get involved in the sport until he was in his 40s.[10]

Today, Colbert seldom discusses his childhood during interviews, and there is a reason. His earliest years were uneventful, nothing special; he was just the youngest kid in a big, Catholic, southern family, just another student at Stiles Point Elementary School. But when he was 10, tragedy struck, and the painful memory and its long-term effect is not something he chooses to reveal frequently.

September 11 is a day of sad remembrance for many Americans because of the events of 2001. But that date has marked a day of mourning for the Colbert family for a much, much longer time.

On the morning of September 11, 1974, Dr. Colbert and two of his sons, Peter and Paul, said good-bye to Lorna and 10-year-old Stephen and drove to the airport to catch a plane. The boys were on their way to the Canterbury School in New Milford, Connecticut. Canterbury was, and still is, a highly regarded Catholic college preparatory boarding school. Peter and Paul, at ages 15 and 18, respectively, were the closest to their youngest brother in age, and he would miss their companionship while they were away at school. Dr. Colbert and the boys boarded the Eastern Airlines plane. The first leg of their journey was a short one, to Charlotte, North Carolina.

The weather in Charlotte was foggy, and the plane was using instrument guidance to come in for a landing. Meanwhile, the pilot and copilot were having a casual conversation, when they should have been watching their instruments more closely. Just a little over three miles short of the Charlotte runway, the DC-9 crashed in flames. Only a handful of the 82 passengers on board survived. James, Peter, and Paul Colbert were among the casualties. The crash sparked the Federal Aviation Administration to put the sterile cockpit rule into effect: once a plane has dropped below 10,000 feet, there is to be no frivolous, unnecessary conversation between the flight officers.[11]

In the blink of an eye, the big family Colbert had grown up in had been tragically reduced. It had lost its strong leader. And Colbert, just 10 years old, had lost his closest brothers. His other siblings were grown or away at university. At home, it was now just Stephen and his mother. Years later, in college, an acting professor would comment to Colbert that serious dramatic roles require the actor to tap into deep emotions, and he did not seem to be able to do this. In an almost casual way, he explained that it may have had something to do with the sudden deaths of his father and brothers—and that, after the accident, alone with his mother, his "main mission became to make her laugh."[12] The professor had been completely unaware of the tragedy.

Stephen coped with the loss in his own way. He recalls returning home on the day of the funeral with a terrible headache. He secluded himself in his room and found a book to read quietly for the rest of the day. That set the pattern for the next five or six years of his life. He immersed himself in reading; his favorites were science fiction and fantasy novels like J.R.R. Tolkien's *Lord of the Rings* trilogy. (Since then, he has read *LOTR* 40 times and can quote extensive passages by heart. Faced with such proof of her husband's geek status, his wife has said, "How do you even know how to breed?")[13] The imaginative worlds of fantasy and sci-fi helped Colbert through that difficult time in his life. "It was a great escape. . . . I'll think about anything you've got other than what there is."[14] Physically, he was present in his elementary and middle school classrooms. But school life, full of childhood rivalries and concerns about popularity and tests, seemed trivial to him. He had a personal knowledge of death that was much closer to home than that of most of his classmates. Colbert was very much in his own little world. "After they died, nothing, I was 10, you know? I was still in school. It was in elementary school. But nothing seemed that important to me.

And so, I had immediately had sort of a, I won't say a cynical detachment from the world. But I would certainly say I was detached from what was normal behavior of children around me. It didn't make much sense. None of it seemed very important. And I think that, you know, feeds into a sense that acceptance, or blind acceptance of authority, is not easy for me."[15]

Making his adjustment even more difficult, Lorna and her youngest son moved from the big family home on James Island to the city of Charleston.

In seventh grade, Colbert recalls being verbally bullied. Though he definitely liked girls, "I got called 'queer' a lot. Just sort of the word that got thrown as a weapon at people when I was a kid and just the most hurtful thing that, I think, the bullies could think of calling you." But when the bullies used the same word against Pat, one of Colbert's friends, the tables turned: Pat announced that he was, indeed 'queer' and offered to kiss the bully to prove it. It defused the situation. And Colbert realized the power of words. "If you don't give power to the words that people throw at you to hurt you, they don't hurt you anymore and you actually have power over those people."[16]

Grieving for his father and brother over many years, Colbert did not apply himself in school but got by on sheer intelligence. One of his friends from his teen years remembers him as "brilliant. He was always the smartest guy in the room, and he was always smart enough not to let you know he was the smartest guy in the room."[17] Colbert's older siblings had attended private secondary schools, and he would as well. When it came time for him to go to high school, he and his mother chose a highly respected all-male institution, Porter-Gaud School, in Charleston. True, its religious affiliation was Episcopalian rather than Catholic, but that was not a deterrent. Boarding school in general, and the Canterbury School in Connecticut in particular, was out of the question, after what had happened to his brothers. In high school, Colbert gradually began to emerge from the shell he had built around himself. In fact, during his senior year he was named class clown.[18]

Colbert does not have fond memories of his time at Porter-Gaud: "I had a very poor high school experience." For instance, one of his teachers was jailed for molesting dozens of students over the years. The man was involved in the school's athletic program, and Colbert recalls a running sick joke among his fellow students: if a boy hit his head on the playing field, this coach would ice the student's groin. (Colbert, incidentally, was not among the school's star athletes.) When the extent of the teacher's abuse became public, the school's headmaster committed suicide. That sort of absurdity would eventually flavor one of Colbert's projects, the Comedy Central series *Strangers with Candy*.[19]

In high school Colbert turned his budding talent for writing into a subversive—and romantic—activity. When he learned that a girl he had a crush on was having difficulty with a teacher, he began writing her letters. In each, the offending teacher would suffer a horrible and violent, James Bondian demise. He wrote poetry, too—just not for the girl. The snuff letters were reserved for her.[20]

In high school, his interest in science fiction and fantasy novels, especially the works of J.R.R. Tolkien, led him to discover role-playing games like Dungeons and Dragons, which he started playing the very week it appeared in the Charleston area. He embraced the games wholeheartedly, even if the association with fellow players labeled him a geek. He still revels in his own geekdom, with a degree of pride. But his interest in role-playing opened up a new avenue for teenaged Colbert: drama. He has elaborated on the similarities between D&D and acting. "It's a fantasy role-playing game. If you're familiar with the works of Tolkien . . . or any of the guys who wrote really good fantasy stuff, those worlds stood up. It's an opportunity to assume a persona. Who really wants to be themselves when they're teenagers? And you get to be heroic and have adventures. And it's an incredibly fun game. They have arcane rules and complex societies and they're open-ended and limitless, kind of like life. For somebody who eventually became an actor, it was interesting to have done that for so many years, because acting is role-playing. You assume a character, and you have to stay in them over years, and you create histories, and you apply your powers. It's good improvisation with agreed rules before you go in."[21]

Or perhaps he inherited the acting bug from his mother, who had a youthful interest in theater but never pursued it. In any case, Colbert got himself involved in his school's dramatic productions. But his role preferences belied his future talent as a comedian. He tried out for, and won, straight dramatic lead roles (his first professional acting gig was in the title role in a serious play called *The Leper*), and that was the direction in which he thought his talent would take him.

In high school, Colbert also discovered that he had a gift for music. He had a good bass voice and sang in the school choir. In his four years at Porter-Gaud, the choir was invited to perform one of Gian Carlo Menotti's one-act children's operas, *Martin's Lie*, at the Spoleto Festival USA, an annual highlight of Charleston's rich cultural calendar. (No, Colbert did not sing the part of Martin, who is a boy soprano.) While he was not in any starring roles, Colbert was also involved in musical theater in high school. Robert Ivey was the ballet and theater director at Porter-Gaud School. He directed a production of *Damn Yankees* and recalls a teenage Colbert, dressed in a baseball uniform, singing in the chorus.[22]

Menotti was not all Colbert could sing. He had a taste for Mick Jagger, too. Colbert and some friends formed a band, which they called Shot in the Dark. While they were not officially a Rolling Stones cover band, Stones tunes were among their favorites. Colbert was, of course, the front man, parading about in a snug, Jaggeresque jersey. A big zero was displayed on the front of the shirt, Colbert on the back. The shirt was not a random choice; even though nearly a decade had passed since the deaths of his father and brothers, Colbert was still in his dark days. The jersey beloved by Shot in the Dark's lead singer had belonged to Peter, one of the boys who had died in the plane crash.[23]

Porter-Gaud has not forgotten its honored, and opinionated, alumnus. It has named its annual debate tournament in his honor.

Upon graduation from high school, Colbert stayed fairly close to home, enrolling in Hampden-Sydney College in Virginia. Hampden-Sydney was, and is to this day, an all-male institution with lots of fraternities. Colbert intended to major in philosophy, which is about the most serious subject you can study—what, how, and why people believe what they have believed through history. The subject may have suited the serious side of Colbert's personality, but Hampden-Sydney did not. "That was like going to college 120 years ago. The languages, a year of rhetoric, all of the great books, Western Man courses, stuff like that. Very regimented curriculum, and a 19th-century emphasis on rhetoric and grammar—and all male. And very conservative."[24]

Hampden-Sydney students actually wore uniform blue blazers. The school was a less-than-perfect fit for teenage Colbert, who saw himself as something of an iconoclast—albeit a "khaki-pants, blue blazer, brass buttons iconoclast."[25] And the opportunities for acting—let alone socializing with girls—in an intensely serious all-male school were somewhat limited. The joy and freedom of being onstage, literally becoming a different character for a few hours, commanding the power to make people cry—or laugh: those things continued to nag at the back of Colbert's mind as he analyzed Plato and Nietzsche. And he began to look elsewhere for a place where he could pursue his deepest interests.

Sometime in 1984, Colbert came to several fateful decisions.

NOTES

1. Edwards, Gavin. "Colbert Country." *Rolling Stone* 986 (2005): 68. MAS Ultra—School Edition. EBSCO. Web. 16 Oct. 2011.

2. Solomon, Deborah. "Funny About the News." *The New York Times Magazine*. 25 Sept. 2005: 18(L). *General OneFile*.

3. Peyser, Marc. "The Truthiness Teller; Stephen Colbert loves this country like he loves himself. Comedy Central's hot news anchor is a goofy caricature of our blustery culture. But he's starting to make sense." *Newsweek*. 13 Feb. 2006: 50. *General OneFile*. Web. 23 July 2010.

4. Strauss, Neil. "The Subversive Joy of Stephen Colbert (cover story)." *Rolling Stone* 1087 (2009): 56. MAS Ultra—School Edition. EBSCO. Web. 13 Oct. 2011.

5. Edwards.

6. Ferguson, D. B. "Exclusive Interview: Rev. Sir Dr. Stephen T. Colbert, D.F.A." *No Fact Zone*. 17 May 2011. Web. 23 July 2011. <http://www.nofactzone.net/2011/05/21/exclusive-interview-rev-sir-dr-stephen-t-colbert-d-f-a/>.

7. Gross, Terry. "A Fake Newsman's Fake Newsman: Stephen Colbert: NPR." *NPR: National Public Radio: News & Analysis, World, US, Music & Arts: NPR*. 24 Jan. 2005. Web. 28 Aug. 2011. <http://www.npr.org/templates/story/story.php?storyid=4464017>.

8. Remnick, David. "Reporter Guy." *The New Yorker*. 25 July 2005: 38. *General OneFile*. Web. 11 July 2011.

9. "Stephen Colbert—IMDb." *The Internet Movie Database (IMDb)*. Web. 19 July 2011. <http://www.imdb.com/name/nm0170306/>.

10. Streuli, Stuart. "Stephen Colbert Challenges you to an Ocean Race." *Sailing World*. May 2011: 30+. *General OneFile*. Web. 12 Oct. 2011.

11. "Stephen Colbert—IMDb."

12. Plys, Cate. "The Real Stephen Colbert: Northwestern Magazine—Northwestern University." *Home: Northwestern University*. Web. 10 December 2010. <http://www.northwestern.edu/magazine/winter 2010/feature/the-real-stephen-colbert.html>.

13. Edwards.

14. Edwards.

15. Schorn, Daniel. "The Colbert Report—CBS News." *Breaking News Headlines: Business, Entertainment & World News—CBS News*. Web. 16 July 2010. <http://www.cbsnews.com/stories/2006/04/27/60minutes/main1553506.shtml>.

16. Stephen Colbert It Gets Better | Colbert Bullying | Video | Mediaite." *Mediaite.com | News & Opinion | Media: TV, Print, Online, Jobs, Ranking*. Web. 28 July 2011. <http://www.mediaite.com/online/stephen-colbert-looks-back-for-the-it-gets-better-campaign-in-seventh-grade-i-got-called-queer-a-lot/>.

17. Mnookin, Seth. "The Man in the Irony Mask; Like Sacha Baron Cohen as Borat, Stephen Colbert so completely inhabits his creation-the arch-conservative blowhard host of The Colbert Report, his Daily Show spin-off hit-that he rarely breaks character." *Vanity Fair*. Oct. 2007: 342. *General OneFile*. Web. 23 July 2010.

18. Brennan, Carol. "Colbert, Stephen (1964–)." *Newsmakers*. Vol. 4. Detroit: Gale, 2007. *Discovering Collection*. Web. 19 July 2011.

19. Gross.

20. P., Ken. "IGN: An Interview with Stephen Colbert." *IGN Movies: Trailers, Movie Reviews, Pictures, Celebrities, and Interviews*. 11 Aug. 2003. Web. 12 Oct. 2011. <http://movies.ign.com/articles/433/433111p1.html>.

21. Rabin, Nathan. "Interview with Stephen Colbert from The Onion's AV Club." *Enter Tony's "Strangers With Candy Companion."* 26 Jan. 2006. Web. 28 Aug. 2011. <http://www.jerriblank.com/colbert_onion-av-club.html>.

22. "Stephen Colbert Sings in Sondheim Show." *The Post and Courier, Charleston SC—News, Sports, Entertainment*. 24 Apr. 2011. Web.

24 July 2011. <http://www.postandcourier.com/news/2011/apr/24/colbert-sings-in-sondheim-show/>.

    23. Strauss.

    24. Rabin.

    25. P., Ken.

Chapter 3

NORTH TO CHICAGO

Colbert, pronounced *Cole*-bert, was sitting on an airplane bound for Chicago. Charleston, Hampden-Sydney College, the major in philosophy, all were behind him; he had enrolled in the renowned theater program at Northwestern University in Evanston, Illinois, 10 miles outside Chicago.

He hoped he was bound for a better education fit for his interests, both curricular and otherwise. "Well, there were girls there, you see. I wanted to study performing—I had decided that the one thing I worked hard at was performing, and it seemed like a hint to me that when I was doing that, when I was working on that, nothing else seemed as important. I was willing to work hard and long, with virtually no reward. Not even anybody coming to the show . . . not a big theater crowd at Hamp-Sydney. And I didn't care. I was so happy to do it. I thought, 'There's a hint. I should do that, then.' I wanted to get an undergraduate degree, and I heard that Northwestern had the best undergraduate program. So, I was happily and luckily accepted."[1]

He was booked into an economy seat in coach. But there was an opportunity to upgrade to business class, and Colbert took advantage of enjoying a roomier seat, more legroom, and better food. He found himself seated next to an astronaut, and they struck up a conversation. Moving to Chicago, Colbert could start a new life for himself, far from South Carolina and people who had known his whole family for years. He could become a new person. And one way to start creating that new person was by giving him a new name. For quite a while, Colbert had been toying with the idea of pronouncing his family name in a different way—a French-sounding Cole-*bear* rather than the Irish version, *Cole*-bert. He ran the idea by his seatmate, the astronaut, and asked his opinion. "I think you know the answer," the astronaut replied. The young man who had boarded the plane as Stephen *Cole*-bert debarked in Chicago as Stephen Cole-*bear*.[2]

Colbert had been thinking about how words and names were pronounced in a larger way, too, for quite a while. To varying degrees, people from South Carolina speak with a southern accent. Regional accents, however, get noticed as soon as you leave that region. And those accents tend to be accompanied by stereotypes. Even as a child, Colbert had noticed that, on television or in the movies, the characters who spoke with a southern accent were almost always the stupid or uneducated ones. He was certainly neither stupid nor uneducated, and he did not want to be perceived that way just because of the way he spoke. He listened carefully to national news programs. You couldn't tell from their accents where the newscasters on the major networks came from. For years, Colbert had been training himself to speak like a newscaster and so lost any trace of his South Carolina accent.

Colbert immersed himself in his work at Northwestern. And that work was intense. He recalls one class as an example of "the lengths to which you would go to try to get the scene right." He and a female student were doing a scene from a Sam Shepard play; the girl had to knee Colbert in the groin. Acting students learn safe ways to simulate dangerous actions, like fight scenes—but the reactions still need to be convincing; pain needs to look real. The teacher was not convinced. While Colbert was still on the ground from the previous strike, the instructor told the girl—a dance major with "legs like oak"—to kick him harder. Misunderstanding, she did—for real, right in the ribs.[3]

Dramatic acting was not the only thing Colbert studied. He was gifted with a good bass singing voice, so he took voice lessons to prepare him for musical theater. He's a decent dancer, too—an ability he's exhibited to great comedic effect more than a few times on television. Ballet was part of Colbert's Northwestern curriculum. Between his innate talent and the top-notch training he was getting, he just might be Broadway bound. In fact, when he tried to explain his love for acting to his mother, Colbert—for once at a loss for words of his own—sang her "Finishing the Hat" from Stephen Sondheim's musical *Sunday in the Park with George*, which he had recently seen.[4] The show is about the painter Georges Seurat and the creation of his most famous work, "A Sunday Afternoon on the Island of La Grande Jatte." In "Finishing the Hat," the Seurat character describes the artistic process as lonely and isolating, yet ultimately absorbing and satisfying ("Look, I made a hat . . . / Where there never was a hat").[5]

Northwestern's theater program ordinarily takes three years to complete; Colbert did it in two. His days were incredibly full, and fulfilling. "I had dance in the morning at 9:00 A.M., I went from dance into water performance class, and another performance class, then into dramatic criticism, then I went into the history of costume and decor, and then into scene design, and then at night I had to do crews for the shows that were running there. They had better facilities than practically anyplace else that I've ever worked professionally. There're huge, gorgeous theaters there with every professional amenity. . . . Everybody there was there because they were very serious about it. So, it got a little bit too serious sometimes, but everybody worked very hard and the teachers were very demanding."[6]

Colbert managed his challenging program while also working two on-campus jobs. One job was in the cafeteria. The other was in the library. This was the mid-1980s. People were beginning to accept that computers were here to stay and could be useful for certain tasks, especially when databases were involved—and a library's catalog is essentially a database. But data needs to be put into the database, which involves a person sitting at a computer, typing information into the appropriate field. Colbert was one of those sitting at a computer, helping to create a digital catalog for Northwestern's huge library.[7]

Chicago has long been known for its improvisational theater. In improv, one actor initiates, or suggests, a situation to his or her partner. The two then pay close attention to each other's cues, both verbal and physical, looking for possibilities for interactions. As for those interactions, when it comes to improv, the odder or less likely, the better. Improvisational actors learn to develop routines on the spur of the moment, often expanding on a random line or occurrence and tapping its potential for comedy. Television viewers can get a taste of improvisational comedy through shows like *Whose Line Is It, Anyway?* (on which Colbert has been a guest).

Colbert described the improv experience in a commencement address he delivered at Knox College in Illinois in 2006.

> There was really only one rule I was taught about improv. That was, "yes-and." In this case, "yes-and" is a verb. To "yes-and." I yes-and, you yes-and, he, she or it yes-ands. And yes-anding means that when you go onstage to improvise a scene with no script, you have no idea what's going to happen, maybe with someone you've never met before. To build a scene, you have to accept. To build anything onstage, you have to accept what the other improviser initiates on stage. They say you're doctors—you're doctors. And then, you add to that: We're doctors and we're trapped in an ice cave. That's the "-and." And then hopefully they "yes-and" you back. You have to keep your eyes open when you do this. You have to be aware of what the other performer is offering you, so that you can agree and add to it. And through these agreements, you can improvise a scene or a one-act play. And . . . by following each other's lead, neither of you are really in control. It's more of a mutual discovery than a solo adventure. What happens in a scene is often as much a surprise to you as it is to the audience.[8]

As a theater student living so close to Chicago, it was inevitable that Colbert would discover some of the city's improvisational theater venues. A friend took him to ImprovOlympic, founded by Del Close and Chama Halpern. There, groups of young comedians would work together to expand short improvisational skits and scenes into a coherent, multi-character, multi-themed play. Close was responsible for inventing some of the techniques that are now standard in improvisational theater. Once a member of author Ken Kesey's LSD-fueled Merry Pranksters, he had battled substance addiction most of his adult life. He finally broke free of his dependence on heroin after the drug-related death of one of his most famous and talented young protégés, John Belushi. Close just missed the rise of faux news programs like *The Daily Show with Jon Stewart* and *The Colbert Report*; he died in 1999. But he definitely understood the potential for satiric comedy in even the most serious world events. Close once said, "It's a grim business, this being funny. Every time you come up with a strong satiric idea, the world tops it. None of our reactionary military characters in the past decade could top the real-life line that came out of Vietnam: 'We had to destroy the village in order to save it.'"[9] It was precisely the sort of ironic statement Colbert would relish a few years in the future.

Colbert was entranced with the process of improvisational theater. He joined a campus improv troupe that called itself No Fun Mud Piranhas. A comember was David Schwimmer, the actor best known as Ross from the long-running television sitcom *Friends*.

Colbert graduated from Northwestern in 1986—more or less. As his family watched, he stepped up to the dean to receive his diploma—and she quietly said to him, "I'm sorry." Inside the diploma cover was a scrap of paper torn from a yellow legal pad with a terse note: "See me." Stephen had an incomplete as a final grade for an independent study course, and needed to make up some credits before he could officially graduate. Midterm commencement came, again Colbert showed up—and again he was denied his diploma, this time because of fines for overdue library books. "They eventually mailed it to me I think. I'm pretty sure I graduated from college."[10]

After graduating at last and leaving Northwestern's campus for Chicago proper, Colbert did what most former fine arts majors do. He rented an apartment with a group of friends, worked at odd jobs, and looked for opportunities to practice his art, preferably for pay. Meanwhile, he continued to explore his developing personality. He still saw himself as an actor of serious rather than comedy roles, so in his day-to-day life he tried to project that image. He came across as a sort of embodiment of Hamlet. But he didn't want to *play* Hamlet; he wanted to *be* Hamlet.[11] "I had to win at being pretentious, being competitive on every level. . . . I was sort of actively, radioactively miserable at people."[12] He grew a beard. His wardrobe consisted of items in variations on a theme of black. He wrote mournful poetry and then stood up at microphones in dark coffeehouses to recite his lines. No one would have mistaken him for a comedian. It wasn't until Colbert was 22 or 23 before "I made a decision not to be actively Hamlet-like and miserable in my daily life, and the decision helped a lot. Living vitally is not easier than living morbidly—it's just better. People are all we've got."[13]

But until that change of heart, Colbert had a very clear vision of his future. "In college, I imagined myself living in New York in some sort of open, large-but-very-sparse studio apartment with a lot of blond wood and a futon on the floor and a bubbling samovar of tea in the background and a big beard, you know, and, you know, living alone but with my beard and doing theater."[14]

Then he got involved in Second City.

NOTES

1. P., Ken. "IGN: An Interview with Stephen Colbert." *IGN Movies: Trailers, Movie Reviews, Pictures, Celebrities, and Interviews*. 11 Aug. 2003. Web. 12 Oct. 2011. <http://movies.ign.com/articles/433/433111p1.html>.

2. Mnookin, Seth. "The Man in the Irony Mask; Like Sacha Baron Cohen as Borat, Stephen Colbert so completely inhabits his creation-the arch-conservative blowhard host of The Colbert Report, his Daily Show spin-off hit-that he rarely breaks character." *Vanity Fair*. Oct. 2007: 342. *General OneFile*. Web. 23 July 2010.

3. Ferguson, D. B. "Exclusive Interview: Rev. Sir Dr. Stephen T. Colbert, D.F.A." *No Fact Zone*. 17 May 2011. Web. 23 July 2011. <http://www.nofactzone.net/2011/05/21/exclusive-interview-rev-sir-dr-stephen-t-colbert-d-f-a/>.

4. "Stephen Colbert: In Good 'Company' On Broadway." *Fresh Air*. 14 June 2011. *General OneFile*. Web. 19 July 2011.

5. "Lyrics, Finishing the Hat Lyrics." *SoundTrack Lyrics Source #1. Any Movie, Musical, TV, Cartoon!* Web. 08 Aug. 2011. http://www.stlyrics.com/lyrics/sundayintheparkwithgeorge/finishingthehat.htm

6. P., Ken.

7. Plys, Cate. "The Real Stephen Colbert: Northwestern Magazine—Northwestern University." *Home: Northwestern University*. Web. 10 December 2010. <http://www.northwestern.edu/magazine/winter 2010/feature/the-real-stephen-colbert.html>.

8. "Stephen Colbert's Address to the Graduates | Media | AlterNet." *Home | AlterNet*. Web. 31 July 2011. <http://www.alternet.org/media/37144>.

9. "Del Close—Biography." *The Internet Movie Database (IMDb)*. Web. 10 July 2011. <http://www.imdb.com/name/nm0167081/bio>.

10. "Stephen Colbert's Address to the Graduates."

11. Peyser, Marc. "The Truthiness Teller; Stephen Colbert loves this country like he loves himself. Comedy Central's hot news anchor is a goofy caricature of our blustery culture. But he's starting to make sense." *Newsweek*. 13 Feb. 2006: 50. *General OneFile*. Web. 23 July 2010.

12. Ferguson.

13. Strauss, Neil. "The Subversive Joy of Stephen Colbert. (cover story)." *Rolling Stone* 1087 (2009): 56. MAS Ultra—School Edition. EBSCO. Web. 13 Oct. 2011.

14. "Stephen Colbert: In Good 'Company' On Broadway." *Fresh Air*. 14 June 2011. *General OneFile*. Web. 19 July 2011.

Chapter 4

DAYS AND NIGHTS
AT THE IMPROV

Second City has become a Chicago institution since its founding in 1959. It is one of, if not *the*, major training grounds for young American comedians. Its teams write and act out skits. They also polish their improvisational skills. Many of *Saturday Night Live*'s stars have risen from Second City's ranks: John Belushi, Gilda Radner, Bill Murray, Tina Fey. Of course there is comedy outside *SNL*, and Second City alumni like Alan Alda, Alan Arkin, and Joan Rivers are among its stars. The original Second City continues to attract and train incredibly funny improvisational comedians. Its young actors practice their craft in front of a live audience each night in a cabaret setting. Besides Chicago, Second City has training programs and theaters in Toronto and Hollywood. It also sends touring companies to theaters across the United States, bringing the experience of improv to people unable to travel to Second City's main stages.

Colbert was still determined to become an actor of serious roles. Much as he enjoyed the challenge of improvisational theater, for a long time he tried to avoid joining Second City's group of comedians in the making. He finally made the leap because he needed the money. He had just returned from tramping around Europe. He was working at an unfulfilling day job assembling cheap futons in the basement of the house where he was living when a friend told him about a job opening at Second City's ticket counter and gift shop. It wasn't quite a commitment to comedy, more answering telephones and selling souvenirs, and Colbert took it. For a long time, he held Second City's record for the most T-shirts sold in a single night.[1] And slowly, his fellow actors drew him away from the souvenir counter and onto the stage.

Colbert was hired at Second City on the same day as Amy Sedaris, Paul Dinello, and the late Chris Farley (later of *SNL*), and they were immediately expected to work together as members of the touring company. Colbert would also serve as understudy to another comedian who would reappear in Colbert's life years later: a guy named Steve Carell.

Colbert's new mates were not quite sure what to make of the quiet, Hamlet-esque young actor in their midst. Sedaris and Colbert had things in common; for instance, although she had been born in New York State, she'd been raised a southern girl in North Carolina, in a fairly large family of five children. Comedy runs in the Sedaris family blood; Amy's older brother is bestselling humor author David Sedaris. Dinello, also from a family of five children, was an Illinois native. He and Sedaris were a romantic couple. For a while, unfortunately, it did not look as if the team would work well together. Sedaris recalls that Colbert took himself far too seriously at first: "I made him laugh onstage once, and he was so mad at me. He went and closed himself in a closet or a bathroom. He was serious and seemed a little aloof, but once we broke him onstage, he just got sillier and a lot more fun."[2] Dinello thought Colbert "was pretentious and sort of cold." In turn, Colbert considered Dinello "just an illiterate thug . . . a Neanderthal." He adds, "Amy likes to say 'we were both right.' Six months later he was my best friend." Dinello was best man when Colbert got married and continues to appear occasionally on *The Colbert Report* as Tad, the building manager.[3]

It took time for Colbert's comic secret to reveal itself. But as he and his castmates tossed about lines and performed pratfalls onstage, the serious shell fell away and the high school class clown—a funny, even silly, Colbert—came to life.

Several times, Colbert had second thoughts about his future in comedy and left the company to pursue serious acting. Each time, Sedaris and Dinello were instrumental in convincing him to return. He finally realized that making people laugh was his true calling when he watched an actress metaphorically crash and burn as she performed a comedy routine. She was playing a coffeehouse singer about to perform a song for the whales. But as she began the routine, she forgot to include that bit of information; she just launched into a weird series of whistles, clicks, and moans. Suddenly realizing her mistake, she stopped and announced, "Oh, this is for the whales!" As they watched the disaster unfold from backstage, Colbert and his friends began laughing hysterically—not *at* the actress in the middle of her truly abysmal performance, but more at the ludicrousness of the whole situation. Afterward, Colbert realized that this kind of joyful camaraderie would not exist in serious theater. Genuinely terrible comedy can be so bad, it's funny—but it would be funny either way. In drama, bad acting can also be so bad it's funny—but in that case, it is unintentional and inappropriate. Backstage during a serious actor's miserable delivery, there might be grimaces, quietly mournful commiseration, consolation, even a bit of despair, and perhaps a little bit of superior gloating—but there would never be hysterical, shared laughter. Colbert chose comedy and has stayed on that track, for the most part, ever since.[4]

Sometimes Dinello and Colbert separated from the rest of their Second City teammates for hilarious comedy club routines of their own. An appearance at one venue, Stella, involved, of all things, bassoons. The two men had talked about a musical sketch based on "The Devil Went Down to Georgia," a fast-paced country classic that describes a truly heated fiddle contest against Lucifer himself. Both Colbert and Dinello played the guitar to some extent, but just being bad guitarists didn't seem funny enough. Bassoons, however—bassoons could be seriously funny (as even Mozart knew well). And neither Colbert nor Dinello had ever even held one before. They went to a music store, rented two bassoons, arrived at Stella with instruments in hand, and performed the routine. First, they tuned up by looking down the instruments, holding them like bazooka guns, tapping on the bells, sensuously licking the reeds, fiddling with the valves. After several minutes devoted to an extended mock tune-up, they began stomping their feet in time and spoke-sang the opening lines of the song, changing the fiddle lyrics to references to bassoons. The audience sounds wild with anticipation for the bassoon contest itself—and both Colbert and Dinello make a valiant effort to get a sound—any sound—out of their instruments. It wouldn't be quite as funny if they weren't both obviously trying so hard! The tuneless result that fizzles out of the two woodwinds sounds like something between a fart and a kazoo toot. Occasionally cracking up, the two musicians soldier on to the end of the song as the rest of the band finally comes to their rescue.[5]

But all was not fun and games for Colbert. He now had strong motivation to establish a career rather than just find a job. In 1990, while attending the Spoleto Festival in Charleston, he met Evelyn McGee. The two had a lot in common: McGee, also a native of South Carolina, was trained as an actress as well. Ironically, as a child she had lived just a couple of blocks away from her future husband, but their paths had never crossed. Just as ironically, she knew comedian Jon Stewart before Colbert did; she had seen some of Jon Stuart Leibowitz's stand-up comedy shows in New York. Before long, Colbert and McGee married and began planning a family.

Second City is an important step for comedians on their way to the top, whether that be *Saturday Night Live*, the Comedy Central network, films, or the stand-up circuit. It is also a place for writers and actors to meet and network. Sedaris saw in Colbert a kindred spirit of sorts; they knew they could work together outside the confines of Second City and produce some funny material. Joining up once again with Dinello, they pitched a television show called *Exit 57* to New York City–based Comedy Central. Consisting of a series of weird skits about five young coworkers, it only ran from 1995 to 1996, but it gave the team valuable experience. And in its brief life of just 12 half-hour episodes, it also garnered some CableACE Award nominations for Best Comedy Series, Best Performing, and Best Writing. (The now defunct Award for Cable Excellence was given annually from 1978 to 1997.) Those talented writers, of course, included Colbert. But the show's cancellation came at a bad time: Stephen and Evelyn Colbert's first child, Madeline, had just been born.[6]

Another comedy project had an even shorter life. *The Dana Carvey Show*, a sketch program, ran for only seven episodes. Nevertheless, its creators included Colbert, plus Second City alum and future *Daily Show* co-correspondent Carell and comic actor Robert Smigel.

Smigel had another opportunity to team up with Colbert. There are very few improvisational comedians who do not find themselves involved with *SNL* at some point in their careers, and Colbert is no exception—for a very short time he was one of its stable of writers. Together with J. J. Seidelmaier, Smigel produced a series of short animated sketches about a pair of superheroes, Ace and Gary. The sketches first ran on *The Dana Carvey Show* but were quickly snatched up by *SNL*. The running gag throughout the series is the unanswered question of whether the dynamic duo is or is not gay—thus the sobriquet "The Ambiguously Gay Duo." Ace was voiced by Colbert; Gary, by Carell. After a four-year hiatus, the sketch returned to *SNL* in an episode that saw the superheroes turned from cartoon characters to flesh-and-blood actors.

In the midst of his comedy activities, an unexpected noncomedic, noncable, network television opportunity opened up for Colbert. ABC's morning light news program *Good Morning, America* hired him as one of its correspondents. He was going to be involved in reporting real news, though the stories he was assigned were on the humorous human interest side rather than headlines. Colbert took the assignment because "I *really* needed a job. . . . I was just doing pick-up work in the New York City area"—not the best situation for a young man with a growing family.[7] But yet again, the job failed to lead to a career for the aspiring actor/comedian. He filmed two stories, but only one was ever broadcast. The segment that made it to the small screen was about a Rube Goldberg contraption competition. Throughout his three-minute coverage, Colbert could not restrain himself from the occasional bit of snarky—though perceptive—sarcasm. It was supposed to be, more or less, a straight piece. It ends up looking like something out of *The Colbert Report*. "They hated me," Colbert said of the experience. "I wanted to do satire, and they wanted someone to be funny like the weatherman was funny."[8] Again, Colbert moved on.

News shows, real and otherwise, had their eye on Colbert. He was tapped to work on Comedy Central's fake news program, *The Daily Show*. The producers lured him on board by telling him that he was "genetically engineered for the show."[9] For Colbert, it was a job, but not one he was enthusiastic about. "I did not believe in the show, I did not watch the show, and they paid dirt. It was literally just sort of—it was just a paycheck to show up."[10]

At that time, the host of *The Daily Show* was Craig Kilborn. Kilborn had primarily worked as a sportscaster prior to his arrival on the Comedy Central scene. The new program and its host received some critical acclaim. But *The Daily Show* was still in search of its stride, and it was far from the hit it would soon become with a new host. In the six months that he worked alongside Kilborn as "The New Guy,"[11] Colbert continued to look for a different, more fulfilling outlet for his unique brand of creativity.

Colbert returned yet again to his old Second City friends Sedaris and Dinello. Sedaris wanted to mine the comedic potential in the after-school special television genre.[12] Like the problem novels being written for teenagers at the time, after-school specials were melodramatic movies focused on a particular teen issue—drug abuse, pregnancy, running away; they were usually aired in the late afternoon, when kids were coming home from school and plopping down in front of the television to recharge. From this concept, the three writers developed

Stephen Colbert reunites with Second City partners in crime Paul Dinello and Amy Sedaris for the opening of Strangers with Candy, *the film spinoff of their Comedy Central television series. (AP Photo/Stephen Chernin)*

the idea for a new Comedy Central sitcom: *Strangers with Candy*. The premise was a quirky one ripe with comic possibilities. Jerri Blank, a woman in her 40s who had dropped out of high school and gone on to a life of drug abuse and prostitution, among other crimes, suddenly appears back in a freshman class, determined to graduate this time. On the show, Colbert played a gay teacher who was in the closet—although everyone in the school was aware of his sexual orientation; Dinello played his partner, the art teacher. The series drew enough of a small but dedicated cult audience to spawn a motion picture. The show ended its run in 2000, and once again Colbert was looking for a worthy vehicle for his talents.

Colbert's big opportunity came with a return to a job that had not worked out too well in the past.

NOTES

1. Plys, Cate. "The Real Stephen Colbert: Northwestern Magazine—Northwestern University." *Home: Northwestern University*. Web. 10 December 2010. <http://www.northwestern.edu/magazine/winter2010/feature/the-real-stephen-colbert.html>.

2. Peyser, Marc. "The Truthiness Teller; Stephen Colbert loves this country like he loves himself. Comedy Central's hot news anchor is a goofy caricature of our blustery culture. But he's starting to make sense." *Newsweek*. 13 Feb. 2006: 50. *General OneFile*. Web. 23 July 2010.

3. "Paul Dinello Dot Net: Biography." *Paul Dinello Dot Net: a Comprehensive Fansite*. Web. 23 July 2011. <http://pauldinello.net/bio.htm>.

4. Plys.

5. "Colbert Dinello—Stella—YouTube." *YouTube—Broadcast Yourself*. Web. 23 July 2011. <http://www.youtube.com/watch?v=a8b85zQ-hHs>.

6. Edwards, Gavin. "Colbert Country." *Rolling Stone* 986 (2005): 68. MAS Ultra—School Edition. EBSCO. Web. 16 Oct. 2011.

7. Gross, Terry. "A Fake Newsman's Fake Newsman: Stephen Colbert: NPR." *NPR: National Public Radio: News & Analysis, World, US, Music & Arts: NPR*. 24 Jan. 2005. Web. 28 Aug. 2011. <http://www.npr.org/tem plates/story/story.php?storyid=4464017>.

8. Edwards.

9. Edwards.

10. P., Ken. "IGN: An Interview with Stephen Colbert." *IGN Movies: Trailers, Movie Reviews, Pictures, Celebrities, and Interviews*. 11 Aug. 2003. Web. 12 Oct. 2011. <http://movies.ign.com/articles/433/433111p1.html>.

11. "Stephen Colbert—TV.com." *TV.com—Free Full Episodes & Clips, Show Info and TV Listings Guide*. Web. 08 Aug. 2011. <http://www.tv.com/stephen-colbert/person/5471/biography.html>.

12. Gross.

Chapter 5

THE DAILY SHOW

In 1999, *The Daily Show* had a new host. Craig Kilborn was gone, chosen to replace Tom Snyder on NBC's *The Late Late Show*. In the anchor's chair was Jon Stewart, an actor and stand-up comedian who had developed a popular but short-lived talk show, *The Jon Stewart Show*, on MTV a few years earlier. Stewart's brand of comedy was quite different from Kilborn's, and the entire feel of the show began to change. Kilborn had focused on silly stories or bad performances by news anchors at small town network television affiliates. Stewart was funny, but he was also incredibly intelligent and well-read. More and more, the show approached real news stories, particularly politics, from the perspective of satire. Stewart and the show's writers monopolized on the many inconsistencies, ambiguities, and unlikely coincidences the viewers of mainstream news could easily overlook. As *Entertainment Weekly* phrased it in an interview with Stewart and Colbert, "Your shows are some of the only ones out there actually digging into archival video to prove when politicians are lying or contradicting themselves."[1] Stewart tackled sensitive topics, from presidential campaigns to 9/11 to the wars in Iraq and Afghanistan. It became possible for people who watched *The Daily Show* to get solid information about the latest news—just from a very slanted, very liberal, bitingly critical, and searingly funny point of view. Under Stewart, the show became a hit, eventually claiming an average of two million viewers a night.

As a literary form, satire has been around for a very long time—since the heyday of fourth-century B.C. playwrights like Aristophanes. Satire involves exposing and ridiculing human vices, or some of the more absurd, illogical, and nonsensical things people—especially people in the public eye—do, in a manner that is supposed to be humorous. Satire works with two conflicting layers of meaning. One layer is direct, or explicit; the audience can assume the satirist really means what he is saying. The other is indirect, or implicit; it could be that the satirist means the exact opposite of what he is saying. Satire is intended to make the audience think critically while they are laughing. And, because those two layers of meaning can get tricky and confusing, it is most successful when the audience is already familiar with the issue under attack; otherwise the humor would be lost on the readers or listeners.

Satire can approach its subject in a number of different ways. For instance, it can be ironic, pointing out incongruities between what a person says and what he or she does. It can be sarcastic, going beyond highlighting ironic inconsistencies to the point of attacking them savagely, with witty, abrasive, cutting plays on words.

Satire uses some standard tools to achieve its goal. Caricature, for instance, exaggerates some noticeable feature of the subject. Editorial and political cartoons make great use of caricature, emphasizing an overweight politician's girth, or a celebrity's nose or teeth or big hair. In a television satire, a caricaturist could highlight someone's unusual speech pattern, or a phrase he keeps repeating, or the way she walks or dresses, drawing attention to that trait until it is seen as funny. Similar to caricature is burlesque, which has more to do with the inappropriate degree of seriousness with which a subject is treated. In a burlesque comedy sketch, a serious topic can be handled in a cute, silly, or lighthearted manner. Or something completely inconsequential can be dealt with in utter, inappropriate seriousness. Travesty is another tool of satire, closely related to burlesque. It means taking something serious and treating or recreating it in an offensively flippant way. Sometimes you hear the term travesty of justice, which means that something so ludicrous has occurred at a courtroom proceeding, it seems more like a mockery than a real trial.

Since the days of Aristophanes, many writers have attacked all sorts of perceived social injustices and incongruities through satire. In 1729, an English writer named Jonathan Swift published an essay in pamphlet form entitled "A Modest Proposal for Preventing the Children of Poor People from Being a Burthen to their Parents, or the Country, and for Making Them Beneficial to the Publick." At the time, Ireland was in the midst of a serious economic crisis. Poor, often unemployed parents were having more children than they could afford to feed, clothe, and shelter. Swift's essay, which presented itself as a serious solution to the problem, was in reality anything but: It advocated treating the children of the poor like sheep or cattle, fattening them up, then slaughtering them to provide another source of meat. Swift is more famous for another work, *Gulliver's Travels*. Now the book is often considered a children's fantasy adventure story, but in fact in its time it was also a satire, attacking various social and political groups represented by the odd lands and races of people Gulliver encounters.

Another author famous for his satire is Mark Twain. Like Swift, Twain can be read on many levels, depending on how familiar the reader is with the social situations being described. *The Adventures of Huckleberry Finn* can be a runaway boy's adventures on the Mississippi River in the company of a slave—or the characters who populate those adventures can be interpreted as caricatures and burlesques and other tools of the satirist's trade.

More in the present, some, though not all, of the sketches on *Saturday Night Live* are satirical. *The Onion* started as a newspaper that made fun of the news, then expanded its range and audience with a website and a television show.

On *The Daily Show*, Stewart had proven that he is a master of satire and its many aspects. Colbert seemed like a perfect fit for the program's new look and feel. "Colbert is part of a long tradition that stretches back to the ancient Greeks," says Michael Rodriguez, who holds a Ph.D. in English literature and teaches a seminar on *The Colbert Report* as satire at Boston University. According to Rodriguez, Colbert, like Stewart, through "skillful use of literary devices, such as syllogism, logical fallacy, burlesque, and travesty, ultimately fosters critical thinking and imaginative engagement, two of the primary skills that writing seminars seek to develop in students."[2]

In 2000, Colbert was invited to return to *The Daily Show*. He was understandably apprehensive. His tenure there with Kilborn had not been remarkably successful. He admitted in an interview for his hometown's newspaper, the *Charleston Post and Courier*, "I really didn't want to do [it] because I hated *Good Morning America*, and I figured it was going to be the same type [of] thing."[3] He was not sure becoming a fake news correspondent for a second time was the right move for his career, but he was persuaded to join *The Daily Show*'s team for a do-over.

Stewart was, and is, *The Daily Show*'s reigning host—in fact, it is now officially known as *The Daily Show with Jon Stewart*. But he has always surrounded himself with correspondents and specialists who play off his humor as characters with their own individual styles of comedy. Not long after Colbert came aboard, Carell (his friend from their Second City, *Dana Carvey Show*, and *Ambiguously Gay Duo* days), Ed Helms, and Rob Corddry would follow as correspondents. Colbert's character needed a background, a personality, and a style of delivery that would be very different from Stewart's, yet would complement it as well, so the two could engage in convincing verbal wrangling on-air.

Jon Stewart, host of The Daily Show, *appears at Comedy Central's benefit* Night of Too Many Stars *with his former "fake correspondents" Stephen Colbert (left) and Steve Carell (center). (AP Photo/Charles Sykes)*

And so was born Stephen Colbert, the character—who should not be mistaken for Stephen Colbert, the actor, despite their identical names. Where Stewart as host is intelligent and well-informed about his topic for the day, and essentially plays himself, Colbert the character is not too bright and fairly clueless on the facts of any given matter yet adamant that his unfounded beliefs are the absolute and unassailable truth. He is, as Colbert (the person) puts it, "a well-intentioned, poorly informed, high-status idiot."[4] He is the embodiment of Benjamin Franklin's wise saying that a little knowledge is a dangerous thing. When the Colbert character gets his teeth into a morsel of knowledge, instead of learning more he twists that little bit to fit his one-sided view of the world. Like Stewart, Colbert the person is genuinely smart. The character Colbert believes he is much, much smarter than he actually is. There is a political slant, too. Where Stewart voices liberal leanings, Colbert is staunchly, unswervingly conservative. Stewart swings towards the Independents and Democrats; Colbert is a die-hard conservative and ultra-Republican. (Colbert the man, by the way, favors the Democrats and is far more liberal than his alter ego.) As for the arrogant way Colbert carries himself when he is in character, he patterned that on newsman Stone Phillips, "because he's the perfect, manly newsman package."[5]

His close involvement with this new version, the Stewart version, of *The Daily Show* forced Colbert to think politically, since politics made up such a huge part of the subjects covered. This was outside of Colbert's personal comfort zone, but something he had to make an integral element of his new character. "I don't really know much about politics. I don't really even like talking about politics much. I don't have an ax to grind. I get disappointed with both sides. But I do like human behavior. So that's what I enjoy talking about, and sometimes politics reflects human behavior. If I thought I had a political point, I'd be in big trouble."[6] Also, the politics espoused by both Stewart and Colbert are surprisingly nonpartisan; their comedy takes aim at the ludicrous, no matter which party is making of fool of itself. "[Stewart and Colbert are] driven more by applying their b.s. detectors to both sides—and, above all, to the media—than by trying to help the good guys win."[7]

Comedy Central recognized Colbert's talent, and the popularity of the character he had created. Before long, Colbert was serving as substitute host of *The Daily Show* when Stewart was on vacation.

Critics and viewers alike sat up and took notice of *The Daily Show* in 2000, a presidential election year. Stewart began a regular segment called "Indecision 2000" to focus on election news. And it soon became obvious that the election of 2000, Bush v. Gore, would be unlike any other. There are always mistakes and missteps, misspoken and poorly chosen words, in the world of politics. But in election year 2000, America was not quite sure who its president was for months and months after the polling places closed. Chads hung on butterfly ballots, and the humble state of Florida made the final call. *The Daily Show* could not have created a more unlikely and ironic scenario, and the writers took full advantage of every opportunity for satire. The program won a Peabody Award that year for its funny, biting election coverage.

Just in case the popularity of *The Daily Show* proved a flash in the pan, Colbert stayed active in other aspects of the television industry, including commercials. Fans of vintage TV ads may remember him as an investigative reporter, a character nearly identical to the one he played alongside Stewart, on the trail of Mr. Goodwrench. The mythical automobile mechanic dubbed Mr. Goodwrench was created by General Motors in 1974 to advertise its policy of equitable, reliable servicing across all GM shops. Until the character's demise in 2010, he had been portrayed in many ways—actor and comedian Tim Allen played him before moving on to fame in the sitcom *Home Improvement*. During an ad campaign that aired in the early 2000s, Colbert visited service bay after service bay, crawling under cars, looking for the *real* Mr. Goodwrench—and milking the resulting ironic humor. In 2010, when GM discontinued the Mr. Goodwrench concept, Colbert did a segment on his show in which he confessed to having murdered the icon on the first day of filming—"If they knew I found him they would have ended the ad campaign! I needed that money!" The body, he added, was hidden where no one would think of looking—inside a blazing yellow Pontiac Aztec,[8] one of the poorest-selling car models in history.

In 2004, as another presidential election loomed, Colbert traveled to Boston to attend the Democratic National Convention as if he were a real news correspondent. The line between fiction and reality, when it came to *The Daily Show*, was blurring. And once again, "Indecision 2004" garnered a Peabody Award for its writers and actors.

Like *Saturday Night Live*, *The Daily Show* was becoming a launching vehicle for television and film stars. Carell left the show in 2004 to star in such films as *The 40-Year-Old Virgin* and *Little Miss Sunshine*, and until 2011 played the pompous boss in the American incarnation of the British TV sitcom *The Office*. Before long *The Office* also welcomed *Daily Show* alumnus Ed Helms into its ranks. Though so far less successful, Rob Corddry also made inroads into network television. The creators and producers of *The Daily Show* recognized that, after the 2004 election, Colbert might also be ready to move on, but Comedy Central did not want to lose him as it had Carell and Helms. He was clearly as talented as Stewart and deserved his own spotlight—but the spotlight on *The Daily Show* was occupied.

And so, in 2005, Ben Karlin (then the head writer for *The Daily Show*) and Stewart sat down with Colbert to talk about possibilities for a spinoff show. As far back as 2002, a sitcom starring Colbert had been discussed.[9] Occasionally, *The Daily Show* had aired fake advertisements that showcased Colbert's character hyping his equally fake TV talk show, which came across like conservative political pundit Bill O'Reilly's Fox network program on a combination of steroids and way too much caffeine. Would Colbert be able to sustain that character for a half hour?

And there was another risk. Colbert, the character, was one thing in small doses on *The Daily Show*, tempered by Stewart's grounding influence. Listening to Jon Stewart for a half hour is a bit like having a conversation with the really smart but likeable guy next door—stimulating, intellectually challenging, humorous, more or less what many liberals would think themselves about issues of the day if they were as clever as Stewart at putting ideas into words. Listening to the Colbert character can be more like getting bashed over the head, loudly and repeatedly, with ideas that are often polar opposites of your own. As Karlin, Stewart, and Colbert debated the character, Colbert cautioned, "I can't be an asshole." And Stewart said, "You're not an asshole. You're an idiot. There's a difference." Idiots can almost be forgiven for some of the nonsense that comes out of their mouths; they do not know any better. As Colbert puts it, "The audience wouldn't forgive Jon for saying things most comedians would want to say. But we can say almost anything, because it's coming out of the mouth of this character."[10]

A *Newsweek* article concurs. "One reason Colbert gets away with being outrageous is that, unlike, say, [the Sasha Baron Cohen character] Ali G, he's not looking to humiliate anyone. Colbert always comes off looking like the biggest buffoon. 'The key to the whole thing is Stephen wearing the character loosely and showing the inherent decency of the man underneath,' says [Jon] Stewart, who is also an executive producer of Colbert's show. 'If you created a character where the audience had to sit back and go, 'Is this man a monster?' you would lose interest.'"[11]

Allyson Silverman, who served as Colbert's new show's executive producer and head writer until 2009, had a distinct vision in mind, too. For her, it would be about finding "out how can satire and silliness live together?"[12]

Comedy Central had so much confidence in Colbert (and in established people like Stewart and Karlin), it approved Colbert's new project without even seeing a pilot episode.[13]

After all that careful planning, would the viewing public be attracted to such an overbearing, smug, arrogant host, even if he were scathingly funny? The moment of truthiness arrived on October 17, 2005.

NOTES

1. Wolk, Josh. "Mock the Vote." *Entertainment Weekly.* 3 Oct. 2008: 34. *General OneFile.* Web. 23 July 2010.

2. Barlow, Rich. "One Class, One Day: Colbert 101 | BU Today." *Boston University.* 11 Mar. 2011. Web. 23 Aug. 2011. <http://www.bu.edu/today/node/12616>.

3. Brennan, Carol. "Colbert, Stephen (1964–)." *Newsmakers.* Vol. 4. Detroit: Gale, 2007. *Discovering Collection.* Web. 19 July 2011.

4. Solomon, Deborah. "Funny About the News." *The New York Times Magazine.* 25 Sept. 2005: 18(L). *General OneFile.*

5. Schorn, Daniel. "The Colbert Report—CBS News." *Breaking News Headlines: Business, Entertainment & World News—CBS News.* Web. 16 July 2010. <http://www.cbsnews.com/stories/2006/04/27/60minutes/main1553506.shtml>.

6. Strauss, Neil. "The Subversive Joy of Stephen Colbert. (cover story)." *Rolling Stone* 1087 (2009): 56. MAS Ultra—School Edition. EBSCO. Web. 13 Oct. 2011.

7. Poniewozik, James. "Can These Guys Be Serious?" *Time* 176.18 (2010): 91. MAS Ultra—School Edition. EBSCO. Web. 14 Oct. 2011.

8. "Stephen Colbert Cops to Killing Mr. Goodwrench." *Jalopnik—Drive Free or Die*. Web. 18 July 2011. <http://jalopnik.com/5691385/stephen-colbert-cops-to-killing-mr-goodwrench>.

9. "Jon Stewart: TV Mogul." *E! Online*. February 15, 2005.

10. Sternbergh, Adam. "Stephen Colbert has America by the ballots: the former Jon Stewart protégé created an entire comic persona out of right-wing doublespeak, trampling the boundary between parody and politics. Which makes him the perfect spokesman for a political season in which everything is imploding." *New York*. 16 Oct. 2006: 22+. *General OneFile*. Web. 23 July 2010.

11. Peyser, Marc. "The Truthiness Teller; Stephen Colbert loves this country like he loves himself. Comedy Central's hot news anchor is a goofy caricature of our blustery culture. But he's starting to make sense." *Newsweek*. 13 Feb. 2006: 50. *General OneFile*. Web. 23 July 2010.

12. Weinman, Jaime J. "The Secret Agenda of Stephen Colbert: In Two Years, He's Turned a 'Daily Show' Spinoff Into a Wacky Sitcom." *Maclean's*. 22 Oct. 2007: 57+. *General OneFile*. Web. 23 July 2010.

13. Edwards, Gavin. "Colbert Country." *Rolling Stone*. 986 (2005): 68. MAS Ultra—School Edition. EBSCO. Web. 16 Oct. 2011.

Chapter 6

A SHOW OF HIS OWN

On that autumn night, Jon Stewart concluded *The Daily Show* with a lead-in for his colleague's new program. Minutes later, with star-spangled, ultra-patriotic fanfare and a catchy signature tune, *The Colbert Report* began. The 54th Street studio was a familiar one for Colbert: It had previously been used for the filming of *The Daily Show*, whose soundstage had just moved a few blocks south down 11th Avenue. Taking its cue from Colbert's pronunciation of his surname, Report is pronounced re-*pore*. The pronunciation is a conscious pun in another way, too: re-*pore* sounds very much like rapport. The word implies "a sense of understanding between the speaker and the listener. . . . [It is a sort of] invitation to the audience to be part of the club."[1] Following the show's rousing introduction, which featured a red, white, and blue palette, lots of flag waving, and a soaring, screaming eagle, Colbert himself finally burst onstage, waving to the applauding audience.

The Daily Show looks a lot like a real news program, with headline features, commentary from the newscaster, reports from correspondents, and an interview. *The Colbert Report,* on the other hand, is patterned on the shows of political pundits like Bill O'Reilly, host of the Fox News network's *The O'Reilly Factor.* News gets discussed, but very much from the biased point of view of the host, who can become loud and bombastic as the spirit moves him. Interviews with guests are dominated by the perspective of the host, who tries his utmost to get the guest to agree with him—despite the fact that guests are chosen for their conflicting and, to the host, erroneous, opinions. The satire on *The Daily Show* is based on the day's news; the target of *The Colbert Report* is more the media than the news it covers.[2] Colbert elaborates further on the difference between *The Daily Show* and *The Colbert Report*: "Jon deconstructs the news. He's ironic and detached. I falsely construct the news and am ironically *attached*. I'm not detached at all. I'm passionate about what I'm talking about. Jon may point out the hypocrisy of a particular thing happening in a news story or behavior of somebody in the news. I illustrate the hypocrisy as a character. That's Jon being Jon and that's me not being me, that's me being the Stephen Colbert guy."[3] Also, "Jon is real and he has fake correspondents. I'm fake and so I like to engage with real things. . . . I like to have . . . like my first guest, instead of having a correspondent come on to have sort of a satirical take on a subject and therefore you explain the news of the day to this conversation, I have the satirical take and I have a real guest on to be my foil and to express what's going on in the news."[4]

The producers of The Colbert Report *show off their Emmy Award in 2008. (AP Photo/Reed Saxon)*

On that first night, Colbert laid the groundwork for what his audience could expect from the new show. "This show is not about me. No, this program is dedicated to you, the heroes. And who are the heroes? The people who watch this show, average hard-working Americans. You're not the elites. You're not the country club crowd. I know for a fact my country club would never let you in. You're the folks who say something has to be done. And you're doing something. You're watching TV. . . . On this show your voice will be heard, in the form of my voice."[5] Here was a character convinced he knew what was on America's collective mind, and what was best for the country, and no one could sway him. In that incredible arrogance lay the roots of Colbert's brand of satire.

Also in the course of that very first installment of *The Colbert Report,* Colbert characterized his made-up pundit character's ideology with a word he made up just moments before trotting onstage: *truthiness.*[6] Introducing the recurring segment known as "The Word" in which incisively ironic comments appear in a sidebar as Colbert comments about an issue, he stated, "I'm not a fan of facts. You see, facts can change, but my opinion will never change, no matter what the facts are."[7] That is the essence of truthiness: It is a truth that is based, not on hard facts and evidence, but on gut emotions and beliefs. Later, in a *60 Minutes* interview, Colbert further clarified, "Truthiness is what you want the facts to be as opposed to what the facts are. What feels like the right answer as opposed to what reality will support."[8] And examples of truthiness were, and still are, running rampant beyond the walls of *The Colbert Report* studio. Just recently, President George W. Bush had nominated Harriet Miers to the Supreme Court to replace Sandra Day O'Connor. When asked whether her qualifications were adequate for the job, Bush replied that, whatever the facts (and the facts indicated that Miers lacked some important qualifications), he knew she was the right choice because "I know her heart."[9]

Truthiness was chosen by the American Dialect Society as 2006's word of the year—around the same time Colbert made *Time* magazine's list of most influential people.[10]

Alongside the concept of truthiness is *wikiality*: "a reality where, if enough people agree with a notion, it becomes the truth."[11] Colbert also invented that word, which has its root in the popular online encyclopedia Wikipedia.com. Wikipedia's content is created by ordinary people *claiming* some measure of expertise in a given subject. Wikipedia can be edited by other ordinary people claiming an even greater measure of expertise in that subject—or just wanting to wreak havoc with the site. On one installment of *The Colbert Report*, Colbert asked Wikipedia users in his audience to alter the facts about African elephants, an endangered species. He claimed he was tired of the rantings of environmental lobbyists, pet targets of many ultra-conservatives. Colbert wanted researchers logging onto Wikipedia to discover that the population of African elephants had, in just the past couple of months, skyrocketed, sweeping them off the endangered list. Fans complied and "corrected" Wikipedia's facts—so quickly and enthusiastically, in fact, that the administrators of the website had to restrict access to all entries referring to "elephant" or "Stephen Colbert."[12]

Like *The Daily Show*, *The Colbert Report* includes some recurring features—"The Word," "Threatdown," "Better Know a District"—and, in each installment, an interview. The guests range from authors to actors to musicians. The interview portion of the show is when Colbert gets to stretch his improvisational muscles; it is, for the most part, unscripted. "I have my plan, and I have three or four questions I know I'm going to ask, but generally speaking, I'm trying to pay attention to what they're doing so that I can ignorantly deconstruct their argument." In other words, Colbert crafts an in-character, improvisational sketch based on their responses. Future complaints about "Better Know a District" aside, Colbert insists he does not "go in like a ninja. I don't seduce [the guests] into a false situation. I say the same thing to all my guests, which is, 'You know I'm doing a character, yes? And he's an idiot, and he will be willfully ignorant of what you know and care about. Honestly disabuse me of what you see as my ignorance, and then we'll have a good time.' There must be something they want out of it, or they wouldn't come. I am not an assassin." Colbert has said that the interviews are his personal favorite part of the program.[13]

The Daily Show with Jon Stewart has its loyal fan base. The fans of *The Colbert Report*, however, are actually organized. They consider themselves members of Colbert Nation and, as the elephant incident indicates, are ready to mobilize at a moment's notice on the go-ahead of their leader, Stephen Colbert (the character)—or completely of their own volition. To Colbert, the very existence of his fan club is a bit of improvisational give-and-take: "[On the show] we joked about the Colbert Nation and then we said, 'Oh s**t, it's real.' That's . . . another improvisational aspect—that discovery is better than invention. We invented the Colbert Nation, but then we discovered it was real. We didn't make it happen, they self-organized it. I love that relationship. We can't always have it, and you can't force that. You just have to acknowledge it." Fans have sent Colbert everything from letters to a Roman suit of armor crafted from leather, complete with a bronze Colbert coat of arms on the breastplate.[14]

And Colbert Nation has real-world clout. A prime example of the power of Colbert Nation is the case of the Hungarian bridge. In 2006, the government of Hungary set up an online poll to determine the name of a new bridge crossing the Danube River in the capital of Budapest. The structure needed a catchier moniker than "Northern M0 Danube Bridge." Colbert caught wind of the poll and asked his followers to get his name onto the ballot. Not only was "Stephen Colbert" listed on the online poll alongside historical Hungarian hero Nikola ubi Zrinksi (and non-Hungarian plays-a-hero-in-the-movies Chuck Norris, as well as neither Hungarian nor heroic Jon Stewart), he won, with over 14 million votes more than Zrinski. (Stewart came in second. Norris was pretty far back.)[15] Success was short-lived, however. The Hungarian ambassador to the United States made an appearance on *The Colbert Report* to break the news that Colbert had failed to meet an important qualification to get the bridge named after him—namely, being dead. (Being Hungarian would have been a plus, too.) The bridge is now officially known as Megyeri Hid.[16]

Colbert Nation also made a valiant attempt to get a section of a NASA space station named after their hero. As with the Hungarian bridge, NASA solicited names for a pressurized module that would create more space (no pun intended) in its space station. Again, thanks to Colbert Nation the most popular submission was "Colbert"; again, the organization was reluctant to name a piece of hardware after a living person (choosing instead the number-eight name on the popularity list, Tranquility). This time, however, there was a consolation prize of sorts; there is now a piece of NASA training equipment, installed within the Tranquility module, called Combined Operational Load

Astronaut T. J. Creamer goes for a jog on the Combined Operational Load Bearing External Resistance Treadmill—otherwise known as COLBERT.

Bearing External Resistance Treadmill: COLBERT.[17] Curt Wieder-hoeft, project manager for the construction of the treadmill, thinks "it's great for NASA that Mr. Colbert got his audience interested in the space station. Comedy Central attracts a lot of younger viewers, and the space program's going to need the next generation's support and interest."[18] Colbert flies a bit lower, too: One of Virgin America's fleet of airplanes is dubbed Colbert Air.[19] (This in spite of the fact that in the middle of an interview, off-air, Richard Branson threw a glass of water in Colbert's face.)

He may not have a Hungarian bridge or a section of a space station bearing his name, but variations on "Stephen Colbert" have been pop-ping up in names of other things—ice cream, for instance. Ben and Jerry's Ice Cream has created flavors named for Grateful Dead founder Jerry Garcia, peace activist Wavy Gravy, and the alternative rock band Phish. There is also Colbert's Americone Dream, a concoction of va-nilla ice cream mixed with fudge-covered waffle cone bits and caramel and advertised as giving its consumers "the sweet taste of liberty in your mouth."[20] In character, Colbert responded that he was pleased to see conservative representation amongst liberals like Garcia and Wavy Gravy; as Colbert the real person, he added that all proceeds from sales of the ice-cream flavor would go toward the Stephen Colbert American Dream Fund, a charitable organization.

Then there are Colbert's critters, some winged, some four- (or eight!-)legged, some flippered. On April 17, 2006, a bald eagle chick hatched at the San Francisco Zoo, part of the zoo's program to increase the population of that formerly endangered species. "Stephen Jr.," an eagle, was adopted by Stephen Colbert Sr., the human, and his exploits since being freed into the wild have been featured periodically on *The Colbert Report.* For a few months the feathered Stephen defected into Canadian territory, and his human dad encouraged border residents to wave salmon around to lure him back into the United States. Like his human father, Stephen Jr. has had a Ben and Jerry's ice-cream flavor created just for him: "Stephen Jr.'s AmeriFlown Dream," like dad's but with the addition of fish-shaped chocolate pieces. In early 2011, Stephen Jr., was spotted in California on a small island near Catalina, where he had first been released. And he wasn't alone: He was keeping company with a female eagle, tagged #24. At five years old, they were ready to start a family and make Stephen Sr. a grandpa.

The eagle is Colbert's signature animal, but it is far from the only creature he has taken under his wing. In 2007, a Stanford University researcher dreamed up the Great Turtle Race in which Internet viewers could follow the progress of leatherback turtles as they migrated from their Costa Rican breeding beach to feeding grounds near the Galapagos Islands. Organizations could sponsor a turtle to pay for the GPS tracking devices used. Coming in second in the race was Stephanie Colburtle, sponsored by Drexel University and named for Colbert, who insisted—facetiously—that Billie, the race's winner, was actually a male who had used a stockpile of ping pong balls to dupe researchers into believing he was a she.

Then there is Colbert's spider. Jason Bond, a biologist at East Carolina University, has been naming newly identified species of spiders after celebrities, including Angelina Jolie, Neil Young, and Nelson Mandela. Colbert's eight-legged namesake is known as *Aptostichus stephencolberti*. His name is also attached to a stonefly native to Chile: *Diamphipnoa colberti*, a six-legged creature appearing in a paper by Bill P. Stark of Mississippi College.

One animal Colbert will probably never see his name attached to is a bear. To say that he is not fond of bears is an understatement. Since the inception of *The Colbert Report*, he has followed incidents of attacks by these snarling "godless killing machines" in a recurring segment called the "Threatdown."[21] It is probably not a coincidence that the nickname of Bill O'Reilly, the ultra-conservative political pundit on whom Colbert heavily based his show and his character, is Papa Bear.

Colbert Nation and its leader have made a mark in the sporting world, too. In 2006, Colbert discovered that the Spirit, a minor league hockey team in Saginaw, Michigan, was in search of a catchy name for its mascot: an eagle, no less, with team colors of red, white, and blue! Colbert Nation mobilized once again, flooding the team's website with votes for the name Steagle Colbeagle. Thrilled with the publicity, the Spirit adopted the name for their giant eagle, who now sports wire-rimmed glasses just like his namesake's. As soon as the newly named mascot was adopted, the team enjoyed a seven-game winning streak. The Spirit's owners also hoped that the Colbert connection would expand its audience into the college crowd, the "demographic making up the majority of *The Colbert Report*'s viewers."[22]

Then, in 2009, a U.S. Olympic team needed help. A Dutch bank, DSB, had pledged $300,000 to sponsor the American speed skating team for the 2010 Winter Olympics in Vancouver, Canada. When the company went bankrupt in a foundering economy, however, no one stepped up to take its place—except for Colbert and his Colbert Nation followers. Ever since the 1980 Olympics in Lake Placid, New York, at which Eric Heiden carried away enough gold medals to fill Fort Knox, Colbert had enjoyed watching speed skating. He encouraged Colbert Nation to come to the aid of one of his favorite sports. And this time, instead of votes, the members came through with donations of money—in the end, even more than DSB had promised. The speed skating team's uniform was emblazoned with the Colbert Nation logo. *The Colbert Report* aired a segment featuring Colbert, on skates, racing against speed skater Shani Davis, who went on to win a gold medal in

Vancouver in the 1,000 meter competition. (Davis drew controversy by publicly calling Colbert a jerk, perhaps because of the character's mocking antipathy toward Canada, in spite of Colbert Nation's sponsorship.)[23] Colbert received even more exposure by appearing, resplendent in spandex, on the cover of *Sports Illustrated,* which to him was "thrilling, ridiculous, because you just don't do that. It just can't be done. And I just love things that are stupidly impossible but somehow happen for the character." In addition, Colbert (with writers and camera crew in tow) followed his team to Vancouver as its official assistant sports psychologist. "I'll be getting in their noodles and helping them work through some of their issues. They've all made a lot of sacrifice to get to this moment, and I'll just remind them of the amazing amount of pressure that's on them and just to never forget that. [There'll be] a lot of yelling. A lot of suck it up and go. Be a man. Stop crying. Stuff like that."[24] While Vancouver was not another Lake Placid for the U.S. team, its skaters did enjoy time in the winners' circle, earning and coming in sixth behind South Korea, the Netherlands, Canada, the Czech Republic, and Germany. Being part of the Olympics was a patriotic act for (in-character) Colbert. "People say America doesn't make anything anymore. We still make war—that's a growth industry for us. But we can't go to war with every country all at once. The Olympics gives us the opportunity to do that."[25]

Jon Stewart didn't have ice cream or a spider named for him. And he had never mobilized his fans to raise enough money to sponsor an Olympic team. Clearly there was something different in the way the public felt about Stephen Colbert's character.

NOTES

1. Gross, Terry. "Bluster and Satire: Stephen Colbert's 'Report': NPR." *NPR: National Public Radio: News & Analysis, World, US, Music & Arts: NPR.* 7 Dec. 2005. Web. 28 Aug. 2011. <http://www.npr.org/tem plates/story/story.php?storyid=5040948>.

2. Gross, "Bluster."

3. Phillips, Jennifer. "Humour, Political Satire, and Ironic Tension Between the 'Real' and the 'Fictional' Stephen Colbert." Thesis. University of Wollogong, 2010. Web. 20 Aug. 2011. <http://www.polsis.uq.edu.au/

docs/Challenging-Politics-Papers/Jennifer_Phillips_Humour_Political_Satire_and_Ironic_Tension.pdf>.

4. "Stephen Colbert: In Good 'Company' On Broadway." *Fresh Air*. 14 June 2011. *General OneFile*. Web. 19 July 2011.

5. "First Show—The Colbert Report—2005-17-10—Video Clip | Comedy Central." *Colbert Nation | The Colbert Report | Comedy Central*. 17 Oct. 2005. Web. 28 Aug. 2011. <http://www.colbertnation.com/the-colbert-report-videos/180903/october-17-2005/>.

6. Sternbergh, Adam. "Stephen Colbert has America by the ballots: the former Jon Stewart protégé created an entire comic persona out of right-wing doublespeak, trampling the boundary between parody and politics. Which makes him the perfect spokesman for a political season in which everything is imploding." *New York*. 16 Oct. 2006: 22+. General OneFile. Web. 23 July 2010.

7. "First Show—The Colbert Report—2005-17-10—Video Clip | Comedy Central." *Colbert Nation | The Colbert Report | Comedy Central*. 17 Oct. 2005. Web. 28 Aug. 2011. <http://www.colbertnation.com/ the-colbert-report-videos/180903/october-17-2005/>.

8. Schorn, Daniel. "The Colbert Report—CBS News." *Breaking News Headlines: Business, Entertainment & World News—CBS News*. Web. 16 July 2010. <http://www.cbsnews.com/stories/2006/04/27/60min utes/main1553506.shtml>.

9. Schorn.

10. "Merriam-Webster Online." *Dictionary and Thesaurus—Merriam-Webster Online*. Web. 06 Oct. 2011. <http://www.merriam-webster.com/ info/06words.htm.

11. Mnookin, Seth. "The Man in the Irony Mask; Like Sacha Baron Cohen as Borat, Stephen Colbert so completely inhabits his creation-the arch-conservative blowhard host of The Colbert Report, his Daily Show spin-off hit-that he rarely breaks character." *Vanity Fair*. Oct. 2007: 342. *General OneFile*. Web. 23 July 2010.

12. Mnookin.

13. Strauss, Neil. "The Subversive Joy of Stephen Colbert (cover story)." *Rolling Stone* 1087 (2009): 56. MAS Ultra—School Edition. EBSCO. Web. 13 Oct. 2011.

14. Strauss, Neil. "Stephen Colbert on Deconstructing the News, Religion and the Colbert Nation | Culture News | Rolling Stone." *Rolling*

Stone | *Music News, Politics, Reviews, Photos, Videos, Interviews and More.* 2 Sept. 2009. Web. 12 Oct. 2011. <http://www.rollingstone.com/culture/news/stephen-colbert-on-deconstructing-the-news-religion-and-the-colbert-nation-20090902>.

15. "Bridge Contest—The Colbert Report—2006-14-09—Video Clip | ComedyCentral." *ColbertNation | TheColbertReport | Comedy Central.* 14 Sept. 2006. Web. 07 Aug. 2011. <http://www.colbertnation.com/the-colbert-report-videos/182256/september-14-2006/bridge-contest>.

16. "Megyeri Bridge / Budapest." *Bridges of Budapest.* Web. 07 Aug. 2011. <http://www.bridgesofbudapest.com/bridge/megyeri_bridge>.

17. "NASA Treadmill Named for Stephen Colbert; Comedian and talk show host gets a consolation prize for his effort to have an International Space Station node named after him." *InformationWeek* (2009). *General OneFile.* Web. 23 July 2010.

18. Siceloff, Stephen. "NASA—Colbert Ready for Serious Exercise." *NASA—Home.* 5 May 2009. Web. 17 Aug. 2011. <http://www.nasa.gov/mission_pages/station/behindscenes/colberttreadmill.html>.

19. "Stephen Colbert | LoveToKnow." *Celebrity Gossip, Oops and News.* Web. 9 July 2011. <http://celebrity.lovetoknow.com/Stephen_Colbert>.

20. "Scoop: Stephen Colbert Gets New Ben & Jerry's Ice Cream Flavor." *Editor & Publisher* (2007). *General OneFile.* Web. 23 July 2010.

21. "Bears." *Wikiality, the Truthiness Encyclopedia.* Web. 12 Oct. 2011. <http://wikiality.wikia.com/Bears>.

22. Wolverton, Jason. "Spirit Name Mascot after Colbert | The Valley Vanguard." 23 Oct. 2006. Web. 17 Aug. 2011. <http://orgs.svsu.edu/clubs/vanguard//stories/1003>.

23. Lewis, Michael C. "Skaters Defend Colbert Against Davis Insult." *Blogs, Commentary and Analysis for Utah: The Salt Lake Tribune.* 7 Dec. 2009. Web. 17 Aug. 2011. <http://blogs.sltrib.com/olympics/index.php?p=7067>.

24. Lederman, Marsha. "Colbert Goes for the Cold." *Globe & Mail* [Toronto, Canada]. 13 Feb. 2010: R1. *Gale Power Search.* Web. 17 Aug. 2011.

25. Dean, Josh. "Colbert on Ice." *Rolling Stone* 1098 (2010): 28. MAS Ultra—School Edition. EBSCO. Web. 16 Oct. 2011.

Chapter 7

THE BUMP

As the popularity of both *The Daily Show* and *The Colbert Report* grew, it became clear that people were watching the faux news programs for more than entertainment. The Comedy Central pair was becoming one of the chief sources of real news for a large number of viewers, mainly young people. A 2008 study by the Pew Research Project for Excellence in Journalism showed that Jon Stewart was among the top five most trusted voices in the news business, placing him alongside such seasoned reporters Dan Rather and Anderson Cooper.[1] As for Colbert, he may have declared *The Colbert Report* a no fact zone, but for some viewers it was quite the opposite.

One scholarly study has looked closely at the political knowledge of young people between the ages of 18 and 29. About one-quarter of the group polled said that they watched Stewart and Colbert regularly; nearly half watched at least occasionally. Less than a third of the group claimed that they never watched Comedy Central's dynamic duo. Then the study compared the people who watched *The Daily Show* and *The Colbert Report* with the general public in terms of political knowledge—for instance, the name of the current secretary of state. Three times as many Stewart/Colbert viewers got that question right.

While Colbert's brand of satire is more oblique than Stewart's—the viewer needs to realize that Colbert is lampooning Republicans while he praises them, for instance, something that might be confusing to some—it is still clear "that regular Colbert and Stewart watchers are significantly more knowledgeable about politics than most other audiences in the same age group."[2]

Colbert himself has a different view of the situation. While he is flattered that people claim to get their news from *The Daily Show* and *The Colbert Report*, he worries that those people might be misunderstanding what he and Stewart are saying and doing. "If they don't get the news story, they're not going to get the joke," he once told Tim Russert of *Meet the Press*. "People say that young people get their news from Jon Stewart and myself . . . but I think they wouldn't get the joke if they didn't know the news already. I think those studies are a little off."[3] He elaborates in another interview: "[*The Daily Show*] is a repackager of news. In that way, I suppose, it is in some ways a valid source. As long as people can understand when we're goofing and when we mean it. If they're not reading the normal news, I doubt that they can. People say, 'Was that story real?' And I've thought, 'Oh, you should really watch the real news before you watch our show, if you can't tell whether our stories are real.' I wish people would watch the real news before they watch our show, because we have two games. Our game is we make fun of the newsmakers, but we also make fun of the news style. They're missing half our joke if they don't keep up with the day-to-day changes of mass media news."[4] He speculates that the shows' political slants give people the idea they're informational, "substantive. . . . But I guarantee you that [they have] no political objective. I think it's dangerous for a comedian to say, 'I have a political objective.' Because then they stop being a comedian and they start being a politician. Or a lobbyist."[5]

The Colbert Report is finding its way into university classrooms as well as into political discussions. Professors are using episodes to teach such literary concepts as irony and satire. Some, like Michael Rodriguez at Boston University, have even developed an entire curriculum around the show; the course culminates in a visit to the Manhattan studio for a taping. Rodriguez's students compare *The Colbert Report* to such classic works of satire as Swift's "A Modest Proposal" and *The Adventures of Huckleberry Finn* by Twain, and Colbert is not found wanting. As mentioned earlier, Rodriguez admires the creative way Colbert's writing staff employs a variety of literary devices to craft the character's trademark brand of satiric humor.[6]

The public may or may not get its news from Colbert. But there is something Colbert's guests get from him: the Colbert bump, "the alleged huge boost in popularity something receives after being mentioned by satirical news host Stephen Colbert of *The Colbert Report*."[7]

For years, the Colbert bump (and its close relative, the Oprah bump) was considered a myth. Then, in 2008, James H. Fowler, who teaches political science at the University of California at San Diego (and is himself a Colbert fan) proved its existence. He found that, in the month following a politician's appearance on *The Colbert Report*, contributions to his or her campaign increase by about 40 percent. But all appearances are not equal; apparently the bump only works for Democrats. For Republican candidates, contributions actually take a dip after a guest appearance with Colbert.[8]

Acknowledging his influence, Colbert cautions that just getting mentioned on the show is not enough for a bump—you need to physically appear on the program and take your medicine in person. And Colbert the character revels in the strength of his bump. "I have to be careful where I point this thing because it's loaded and it is powerful. For Pete's sake, I talked about Hitler, Lindsay Lohan, and chlamydia. I was not giving them the bump. That was just sweeps week."[9]

Not everyone is willing to do what it takes to get the Colbert bump. There are risks involved.

Colbert has said that he holds his character in check when he is interviewing scientists and some authors. But when it comes to politicians, no holds are barred. Colbert always asks his guests some outrageous questions, and he gets especially creative with those in the political arena.

When *The Colbert Report* first began, one of its recurring segments was "Better Know a District," in which Colbert interviews a member of Congress, often in his or her office. It was projected as a 434-part series—the number of congressional districts in the 50 states plus the District of Columbia. At first, the interviews seemed like a good way for members of Congress to get a bit of free media coverage and perhaps to even enjoy a Colbert bump. In 2006, 40 "Better Know a District" segments aired. But once congressmen and women saw themselves and their colleagues on the show, many had second thoughts about joining the ranks. They often had little idea of what the interview would look like once it aired, since a couple of minutes were cobbled together from hours of talk in front of the cameras. All that footage was edited to focus on the funniest moments, or patched together out of context to make it look like the congressman had said something ridiculous or incriminating. Or sometimes, he or she just tried to respond to Colbert's increasingly absurd questions. As of mid-2011, only a quarter of the districts and their congressional representatives have been profiled.

In a notorious "Better Know a District" installment, Colbert questioned Representative Jack Kingston of Georgia at length about his experience as an African American. It is quite obvious in the televised interview that Kingston is unmistakably white. Born in Texas, the young Kingston and his parents lived for a few years in Ethiopia before returning to the United States. It's a minor detail in his life, but it's the one Colbert focused on because it created such great irony.

On June 14, 2006, Colbert met with another representative from Georgia, Republican Lynn Westmoreland from the state's 8th District. Westmoreland was sponsoring a bill that required the Ten Commandments to be displayed in Congress. Colbert asked the congressman to name the Commandments. Westmoreland got as far as three before floundering and giving up.[10]

In November 2005, Colbert's guest was Stephanie Tubbs Jones, who represented Ohio's 11th District. They talked at length about Abraham Lincoln, but Colbert also noted the number of astronauts born in her state. "Twenty-two astronauts were born in Ohio. What is it about your state that makes people want to flee the earth?" he queried.[11] When Jones died suddenly of a brain aneurysm three years later, her appearance on the then-new *The Colbert Report* and her flawless comedic timing in the face of such an interrogator were noted in her obituaries.

On Colbert's July 20, 2006, show, the subject of "Better Know a District" was Democratic representative Robert Wexler of Florida's 19th District. Wexler was running uncontested for reelection—in other words, he couldn't lose. In the course of the interview, Colbert suggested, "Let's say some things that would really lose the election for you if you were contested." Wexler was posed with a fill-in-the-blank question: "I enjoy cocaine because . . ." Colbert coached him to respond, very seriously, in a way that would jeopardize the election if there were any way he could lose. After stifling his laughter, Wexler finally replied, "I enjoy cocaine because it's a fun thing to do." Colbert's next question: "I enjoy the company of prostitutes for the following reasons . . ." And again, Wexler replied, "Because it's a fun thing to do. . . . If you combine the two things together it's probably even more fun." "Wow!" Colbert responded. "We'd better finish this interview quick because I'm not sure how long you're gonna be in Congress."[12] When he next came up for reelection, Wexler did have an opponent, but his appearance on *The Colbert Report* had not hurt him; he won. Wexler finally resigned his seat in 2010 to become president of the S. Daniel Abraham Center for Middle East Peace—quite a post for a man who admitted to using cocaine and consorting with prostitutes, albeit jokingly, on national television.

Just a week later, on July 27, Colbert met his match in Eleanor Holmes Norton, representative for the District of Columbia, who deflected his attempts at humor and proceeded to give him a civics lesson. When Norton proudly announced that she'd been born in Washington, D.C., Colbert countered, "Then you can never be president," since one of the criteria is having the United States as one's place of birth. Challenged by Colbert regarding the non-state status of the district, Holmes Norton condescendingly responded, "You are the *first* to suggest that the nation's capital is not in the United States." Growing increasingly aggressive, Norton asked about the pronunciation of Colbert's name and his ancestry. When he replied that his family was from the United States, she said, quite firmly, "Anyone who pronounces COLE-bert Cole-BEAR is *not* from the United States!" Colbert's philosophy background from Hampden-Sydney came in handy as he and Holmes Norton continued their game of twisted logic. And as the exchange became more and more heated and Holmes Norton was clearly getting angry, Colbert observed, "You see now why you don't get a vote?" The conversation turned to gayness and sexual harassment; Norton turned on Colbert and accused him of being nothing more than "a plain vanilla man who is asking me questions."[13] Despite—or maybe because of—their consistently lively sparring, Holmes Norton has made fairly frequent return appearances on *The Colbert Report*.

Representative Mark Udall of Colorado talked with Colbert about his attempts to climb Mount Everest. Three times, he failed to summit. Colbert said to Udall, "Don't take this the wrong way, but doesn't that make you a quitter?" Udall replied, "I don't think the Q word applies to me. Maybe the L word." (He was probably referring to loser.) Not missing a beat, Colbert responded, "You do know the L word is 'lesbian.'"[14] Udall was not amused. Others, however, are willing to risk a bit of foolishness for the honor of the bump. As Republican representative Jason Chaffetz of Utah said of his 2009 interview, Colbert is "a good, fun guy if you're OK with getting made fun of. You never know how you're going to respond to a question. . . . But," Chaffetz qualified, "I like self-deprecating humor." Members of Congress have begun to warn their colleagues about the risks of doing a "Better Know a District" segment. Aides turn down *The Colbert Report* requests, unless they are for a live appearance, which is less likely to be heavily edited. Speaker of the House Nancy Pelosi is a fan of the show but adds, "I watch it all the time, and I think, 'Why would anybody go on there?'"[15] Given his reputation, Pelosi—who has often been the butt of Colbert's jokes but put off actually appearing on the show until February 2012—doubts he will be able to reach his goal of 434 districts.[16]

President Barack Obama has yet to appear on *The Colbert Report* in person, although he has spoken to Colbert via satellite. First Lady Michelle Obama, however, has been Colbert's guest, as has former First Lady and current secretary of state Hillary Clinton.

Another politician who has never appeared in the flesh on *The Colbert Report* is Sarah Palin, Republican John McCain's vice-presidential running mate in 2008. (Palin did include a taped cameo shout-out to her son in the military during the week of shows Colbert broadcast from Iraq in 2009.) With the 2012 election and its associated campaigns becoming a topic of serious conversation as 2011 wore on, Colbert again turned his attention to the frontrunners and the big issues. Palin's many verbal faux pas—which were all the more noticeable because she was very outspoken and eager to speak to the press—may have contributed to McCain's loss to Obama. But Palin had gotten a taste of high stakes politics and found it to her liking. While resigning as governor of Alaska, she nevertheless involved herself in a conservative, libertarian offshoot of the Republican Party that called itself the

Tea Party. Her 2008 candidacy over, she was still in the public eye—and still putting her foot in her mouth with regularity.

In June 2011, Palin was promoting the Tea Party in Boston, Massachusetts, touring historic sites. She was particularly impressed by the story of patriot Paul Revere, who, according to her, "warned the British that they weren't going to be taking away our arms, by ringing those bells and making sure, as he is riding his horse through town, to send those warning shots and bells, that we were going to be secure and we were going to be free."[17] Palin's truthiness was in the right place. She got the name, the nationalities, and the horse right; the rest, with its libertarian slant, not so much. Almost immediately, historians chimed in with their comments on the inaccuracies in Palin's description. And almost as quickly, in a perfect example of wikiality, her supporters tried to change the Wikipedia entry on Paul Revere.

One of the things Palin got wrong had to do with warning shots. Historians corrected her by reporting that, at the time, guns were muzzle loaded. It took a long time to prepare the gun for firing, making the whole concept of a warning shot both a waste of time and downright dangerous: after you had fired your warning, your opponent could easily retaliate while you were painstakingly reloading for the money shot.

Tom Purcell, executive producer, caught that detail about the warning shot, too, and, in the course of a meeting, insisted it was a historical anachronism, it couldn't be done.[18] And so, on the June 6, 2011, show, "For those who say it's implausible for Revere to have ridden a horse while ringing a bell and firing multiple warning shots from a front-loading musket," Colbert announced, "prepare to eat historical re-enactment."[19] In place of a live horse, Colbert's segment producers, Matt Lappin and Adam Wager, procured the sort of mechanical metal pony children pay a few cents to bounce around on, usually found outside shopping centers. Colbert mounted the horse wearing a tricorn hat and sporting a musket and the requisite powder horns. Once fed a coin, the mechanical pony went into full gallop. Colbert successfully mimicked firing off his initial shot. The tough part was reloading—while the horse lurched on. Powder and shot flew everywhere but into the musket's barrel. Colbert finally resorted simply to ringing the bell clutched in his left hand until the pony chugged to a stop. "Let's just say it can't be done," Colbert concluded.[20]

Those in the political limelight are not the only people eligible for the bump; nonpoliticians, too, enjoy the exposure they can get through five minutes of sparring with Colbert at the round table. Many of Colbert's guests are authors. (Incidentally, Colbert admits that, while he is still an avid reader, he simply does not have time to read the books he discusses with his guests.)[21] In 2009, author Neil Gaiman won the Newbery Award for *The Graveyard Book*. The Newbery Award is given annually by the American Library Association to honor the best children's book published by an American author in the previous year. Gaiman was already a respected writer of graphic novels and adult fantasies full of a Colbert-esque sense of dark but whimsical humor. During the awards ceremony at ALA's annual conference in Chicago that year, Gaiman stood at the podium to give his speech. He mentioned his daughters, whom he had finally impressed "by having been awarded the Newbery Medal." But there was something his son found much, much cooler. "I impressed my son even more by defending the fact that I had won the Newbery Medal from the hilarious attacks of Stephen Colbert on *The Colbert Report*, so the Newbery Medal made me cool to my children. This is as good as it gets. You are almost never cool to your children."[22]

Scientists are glad to take any bump they can get from Colbert, too. Sean Carroll, a professor at California Institute of Technology, appeared on *The Colbert Report* in July 2010. A physicist, he talked about the book he had recently published, in which he speculates about the nature of time and the existence of multiple universes. Heavy stuff. Carroll praised both Colbert and Stewart "for understanding that science is fascinating and fun, not off-putting and work." Jody Baumgartner, who teachers political science at East Carolina University and has written about the effect of faux news programs like *The Daily Show* and *The Colbert Report* on public perceptions, agrees. "It seems to me as if any 'risk' for scientists appearing on these programs is minimal. Both Stewart and Colbert seem to be genuinely respectful of their science guests, even if they do engage in dialogue that is intended to generate laughs."[23] (It must be noted that Colbert admits to dialing down the comic intensity of his character when his guest is a theoretical scientist.)[24]

But in the spring of 2006, *The Colbert Report* was not even a year old, and the existence of a Colbert bump was speculation at best. And Colbert was called upon to give the Colbert treatment to the ultimate sub-ject: then-president of the United States George W. Bush. But would he give the president a much-needed bump in public ratings—or would his speech metaphorically bump Bush under a bus?

NOTES

1. Rose, David. "Stewart, Colbert Influence Politics through Com-edy—Opinion." *Kansas State Collegian—Kansas State University.* Web. 31 July 2011. <http//www.kstatecollegian.com/opinion/stewart-colbert-influence-politics-through-comedy-1.2385706>.

2. Baumgartner, Jody C., and Jonathan S. Morris. "One 'Nation,' under Stephen? The Effects of The Colbert Report on American Youth." *Journal of Broadcasting & Electronic Media* 52.4 (2008): 622+. *General OneFile.* Web. 22 July 2010.

3. "The Real Stephen Colbert (Out of Character)—YouTube." *YouTube—Broadcast Yourself.* Web. 23 July 2011. <http://www.youtube.com/watch?v=DNvJZCFpdp8>.

4. P., Ken. "IGN: An Interview with Stephen Colbert." *IGN Movies: Trailers, Movie Reviews, Pictures, Celebrities, and Interviews.* 11 Aug. 2003. Web. 12 Oct. 2011. <http//movies.ign.com/articles/433/433111p1.html>.

5. Solomon, Deborah. "Funny About the News." *New York Times Magazine.* 25 Sept. 2005: 18(L). *General OneFile.*

6. Barlow, Rich. "One Class, One Day: Colbert 101 | BU Today." *Boston University.* 11 Mar. 2011. Web. 23 Aug. 2011. <http//www.bu.edu/today/node/12616>.

7. "The Great Turtle Race: Tracking a Leatherback | The News-Sentinel—Fort Wayne IN." *The News-Sentinel—FRONTPAGE-Fort Wayne IN.* 12 June 2008. Web. 31 July 2011. <http://www.news-sentinel.com/apps/pbcs.dll/article?AID=/20080612/NEWS/806120307>.

8. "Measuring the 'Colbert Bump': Do Politicians Raise More Funds After Appearing on The Colbert Report Comedy Show?" *US Newswire.* 13 Aug. 2008. *General OneFile.* Web. 28 July 2011.

9. "Herman Cain Claims the Colbert Bump—The Colbert Re-port—2011–11–05—Video Clip | Comedy Central." *Colbert Nation |*

The Colbert Report | Comedy Central. 11 May 2011. Web. 13 Sept. 2011. <http://www.colbertnation.com/the-colbert-report-videos/386084/may-11-2011/herman-cain-claims-the-colbert-bump>.

10. "Better Know a District—Georgia's 8th—Lynn Westmoreland—The Colbert Report—2006–14–06—Video Clip | Comedy Central." *Colbert Nation | The Colbert Report | Comedy Central.* 14 June 2006. Web. 11 Sept. 2011. <http://www.colbertnation.com/the-colbert-report-videos/70730/june-14-2006/better-know-a-district—georgia-s-8th—lynn-westmoreland>.

11. "Better Know a District—Ohio's 11th—Stephanie Tubbs Jones—The Colbert Report—2005–03–11—Video Clip | Comedy Central." *Colbert Nation | The Colbert Report | Comedy Central.* 3 Nov. 2005. Web. 11 Sept. 2011. <http://www.colbertnation.com/the-colbert-report-videos/24729/november-03-2005/better-know-a-district—ohio-s-11th—stephanie-tubbs-jones>.

12. "Better Know a District—Florida's 19th—Robert Wexler—The Colbert Report—2006–20–07—Video Clip | Comedy Central." *Colbert Nation | The Colbert Report | Comedy Central.* 20 July 2006. Web. 11 Sept. 2011. <http://www.colbertnation.com/the-colbert-report-videos/72021/july-20-2006/better-know-a-district—florida-s-19th—robert-wexler>.

13. "Better Know a District—District of Columbia—Eleanor Holmes Norton—The Colbert Report—2006–27–07—Video Clip | Comedy Central." *Colbert Nation | The Colbert Report | Comedy Central.* 27 July 2006. Web. 11 Sept. 2011. <http://www.colbertnation.com/the-colbert-report-videos/72238/july-27-2006/better-know-a-district—district-of-columbia—eleanor-holmes-norton>.

14. "Better Know a District—Colorado's 2nd—Mark Udall—The Colbert Report—2005–16–11—Video Clip | Comedy Central." *Colbert Nation | The Colbert Report | Comedy Central.* 16 Nov. 2005. Web. 11 Sept. 2011. <http://www.colbertnation.com/the-colbert-report-videos/59467/november-16-2005/better-know-a-district—colorado-s-2nd—mark-udall>.

15. "Congress Cools on Stephen Colbert—Erika Lovley and Marin Cogan—Politico.com." *Politics, Political News—Politico.com.* Web. 11 Sept. 2011. <http//www.politico.com/news/stories/0910/42929.html>.

16. "Better Know a District—New Members of Congress at the Kennedy School—The Colbert Report—2006–12–12—Video Clip | Comedy Central." *Colbert Nation | The Colbert Report | Comedy Central.* 12 Dec. 2006. Web. 12 Oct. 2011. <http://www.colbertnation.com/the-colbert-report-videos/79466/december-12-2006/better-know-a-district—new-members-of-congress-at-the-kennedy-school>.

17. "How Accurate Were Palin's Paul Revere Comments?" *All Things Considered.* 6 June 2011. *General OneFile.* Web. 22 July 2011.

18. "Stephen Colbert: In Good 'Company' On Broadway." *Fresh Air.* 14 June 2011. *General OneFile.* Web. 19 July 2011.

19. "Stephen Colbert Reenacts Sarah Palin's Version of Paul Revere's Ride (VIDEO)." *Television | TV | Show Guides | TV Series Online | AOL Television.* Web. 22 July 2011. <http//www.aoltv.com/2011/06/07/colbert-reenacts-sarah-palin-paul-revere-ride-video/>.

20. "Stephen Colbert: In Good 'Company.'"

21. Strauss, Neil. "Stephen Colbert on Deconstructing the News, Religion and the Colbert Nation | Culture News | Rolling Stone." *Rolling Stone | Music News, Politics, Reviews, Photos, Videos, Interviews and More.* 2 Sept. 2009. Web. 12 Oct. 2011. <http://www.rollingstone.com/culture/news/stephen-colbert-on-deconstructing-the-news-religion-and-the-colbert-nation-20090902>.

22. Gaiman, Neil. "Newbery Medal Acceptance." *The Horn Book Magazine* 85.4 (2009): 343+. *General OneFile.* Web. 23 July 2010.

23. "King of the Road." *The Hotline* (2010). *General OneFile.* Web. 22 July 2010.

24. "The Real Stephen Colbert (Out of Character)."

Chapter 8

THE INFAMOUS WHITE HOUSE CORRESPONDENTS' DINNER

Each year in April, the president of the United States hosts a White House Correspondents' Dinner, at which the people at the top of the political ladder and the members of the press who cover their stories rub shoulders. The 2006 dinner was held on the evening of April 29. Besides journalists and politicians, a smattering of celebrities is always invited as well: at that particular dinner one could see actor George Clooney, actress Morgan Fairchild, football star Ben Roethlisberger. Altogether there were 2,700 people present. Traditionally, entertainment at the dinner is provided by a comedian whose routines feature a political slant. In 2006, probably in recognition of the popularity of his new show and his persona's *apparent* support of the Bush administration, Mark Smith, president of the White House Correspondents' Association, selected Colbert. (Afterward Smith admitted he was not all that familiar with Colbert's work.)[1] What Colbert delivered was totally in character, yet totally unexpected and heavily criticized on all sides.

In an interview Colbert did shortly before the big day, he quipped, "I'm so excited I'm going to levitate."[2] There would indeed be a reference to levitation of another kind during the dinner itself—though it would be to the Hindenburg disaster.

On that fateful night, stepping up to the microphone, Colbert lost no time making his first strike. After a few minutes of patter, a mash-up from several of his shows, Colbert looked at President Bush and announced,

> I stand by this man. I stand by this man, because he stands for things. Not only for things, he stands on things, things like aircraft carriers and rubble and recently flooded city squares. And that sends a strong message that no matter what happens to America, she will always rebound with the most powerfully staged photo-ops in the world.

Bush was in the middle of his final term as president, and the public's opinion of his administration was at a low point. Invoking truthiness with a line repeated from one of his shows, Colbert admonished the conservative Republican president to ignore reality, which has a liberal bias anyway. Truthiness was a recurring theme throughout Colbert's routine: "When the president decides something on Monday, he still believes it on Wednesday—no matter what happened Tuesday. Events can change; this man's beliefs never will."

To counteract the problems in the White House, there had recently been some major staff changes, which had been criticized as being as futile as the proverbial rearranging the deck chairs on the *Titanic*. Colbert responded that the administration was "soaring, not sinking," so that "if anything, they are rearranging the deck chairs on the *Hindenburg*."

The president's role in the ongoing war in the Middle East was another of Colbert's targets that night. "I believe that the government that governs best is the government that governs least, and by these standards we have set up a fabulous government in Iraq."

Since this was a dinner for political correspondents, Colbert took aim at the journalists present, too. Invoking truthiness again ("I give people the truth, unfiltered by rational argument. I call it the No Fact Zone."), he attacked "the liberal media who are destroying this country, except for Fox News. Fox believes in presenting both sides of the story—the president's side and the vice president's side." He later added, "Over the last five years you people were so good, over tax cuts, WMD intelligence, the effect of global warming. We Americans didn't want to know, and you had the courtesy not to try to find out. Those were good times, as far as we knew."[3]

For a very short time, President Bush and wife Laura tried to smile, but as the sharp-tongued irony continued, the good humor dissipated. As Colbert left the podium, Bush gave him a curt nod and said, "Well done," but later barely shook his hand. (According to Jon Stewart, that "well done" referred "to how he would like to cook Stephen's hide on the barbecue.")[4] Throughout his routine, Colbert had been unaware that something was not quite right, since there had been laughter in the room. It was not until he returned to his seat that he realized no one was making eye contact with him.[5]

Afterward, politicians and journalists alike were angry and confused by Colbert's "controversial, possibly very funny, possibly horribly unfunny, possibly bravely patriotic, and possibly near-seditious monologue."[6] Even Allyson Silverman, a *The Colbert Report* writer who had been in the audience, half joked that she was now "afraid for my life."[7]

A moment from the White House Correspondents' Dinner, which has gone down in infamy. (AP Photo/ Haraz N. Ghanbari)

But what, really, had people expected? Colbert, the character, might sound on his television show like he was a supporter of the Bush administration, especially when he waxed patriotic. But if you listened carefully to what he was saying, every positive statement hid a sharp, incisive thorn of irony. When Colbert the character was invited to speak, he spoke in character, and that was exactly what he delivered at the White House Correspondents' Dinner.

C-SPAN and YouTube quickly provided television and Internet viewers access to the scathing speech, so that in the space of two days it was heard, not by an elite 2,700, but by over two and a half million people around the world. Reactions varied. The *Washington Post*'s Richard Cohen called Colbert "not just a failure as a comedian but rude." Chris Lehman of the *Observer* concurred: "The material came off as shrill and airless." On the other hand, in an editorial printed in the *New York Times*, a Colbert fan wondered, "If his performance wasn't funny, perhaps it's because he wasn't joking."[8] Another person who enjoyed the controversial speech was Senator John Kerry, who had been present at the dinner and appreciated the humor, as he revealed in a video-taped backstage comment while preparing for his own appearance on *The Colbert Report*.[9]

Colbert's reaction to his possibly overdone roast? "I was there to do some jokes. I was there to do what I do. I expected maybe a whiff of brimstone. A soupçon of scandal. Did I expect this to be a line in the sand for people? No, absolutely not."[10]

NOTES

1. Sternbergh, Adam. "Stephen Colbert has America by the ballots: the former Jon Stewart protégé created an entire comic persona out of right-wing doublespeak, trampling the boundary between parody and politics. Which makes him the perfect spokesman for a political season in which everything is imploding." *New York*. 16 Oct. 2006: 22+. *General OneFile*. Web. 23 July 2010.

2. Peyser, Marc. "The Truthiness Teller; Stephen Colbert loves this country like he loves himself. Comedy Central's hot news anchor is a goofy caricature of our blustery culture. But he's starting to make sense." *Newsweek*. 13 Feb. 2006: 50. *General OneFile*. Web. 23 July 2010.

3. Colbert, Stephen. *I Am America (And So Can You!)*. New York: Grand Central Pub., 2007, pp. 223–224.

4. Dowd, Maureen. "America's Anchors. (cover story)." *Rolling Stone* 1013 (2006): 52. MAS Ultra—School Edition. EBSCO. Web. 13 Oct. 2011.

5. Sternbergh.

6. "Charlie Rose—A Conversation with Comedian Stephen Colbert." *Charlie Rose—Home*. 8 Dec. 2006. Web. 23 Aug. 2011. <http://www.charlierose.com/view/interview/93>.

7. Sternbergh.

8. Sternbergh.

9. "The Colbert Report: A Rare Behind-the-Scenes Look—YouTube." *YouTube—Broadcast Yourself*. Web. 23 July 2011. <http://www.youtube.com/watch?v=DfiL2hpnmZ0>.

10. Sternbergh.

Chapter 9

HAT IN THE RING

As they say, you don't criticize someone's bad job if you can't do better yourself. Colbert had ripped into the press and the president with ferocity. He already was a journalist—fake, perhaps, but respected by his public. But was he ready to tackle the biggest responsibility in the country?

He had Colbert Nation to support him. His loyal fans had tried—and occasionally failed—to get their hero's named affixed to inanimate objects. Would they be more successful when it came to America's ultimate popularity contest: the 2008 presidential race?

In the course of his October 16, 2007, show, Colbert made a momentous announcement: he was declaring himself a presidential candidate. As a beginning, he would try to get himself onto the ballot for the South Carolina primary. Though he had not lived there for many years, it was the state of his birth and childhood; his wife, too, was a native South Carolinian. Colbert could be considered a native son. As his running mate, he was considering (a) himself; (b) Russian President Vladimir Putin; (c) Mike Huckabee, the governor of Arkansas.[1] During an interview with *Meet the Press*'s Russert, Colbert explained why he was concentrating on South Carolina:

> I believe that it's the greatest state of the union, I believe there are things that—I believe I can make a difference there. I think it is time to focus on South Carolina. Florida tried to jump South Carolina's primary date for both the Republicans and the Democrats. I want to put the focus back on South Carolina. I want it to be a permanent thing. I don't want Iowa and New Hampshire to be the only people in the United States who get to control who is a bellwether state. And if Iowa and New Hampshire don't like that, they can take some of that Iowa corn and stick it right up their Dixville Notch.[2]

Comedians running for president are nothing new in American politics or popular culture. In nearly every election from 1968 through the 1990s, for instance, Pat Paulsen, a poker-faced regular on the popular 1960s comedy revue *Rowan and Martin's Laugh-In*, had declared his candidacy. But these people had never been taken seriously; they were comedians, and their election bids were seen as jokes.

> Previous comedians who pretended to throw their hats into the U.S. presidential ring seemed to do so . . . in order to make a larger point, in addition to providing giggles along the way. Pat Paulsen . . . reminded us that speechifying politicos can be bombastic, bumbling, soporific, and tone-deaf—lessons that Michael Dukakis, Al Gore, and John Kerry should have taken to heart. Wavy Gravy, in his cross-country 'Nobody for President' campaign (in 1976, 1980, and 1984), gave humorous voice and a protest alternative to the frustration many citizens felt and still feel about our national politics, namely that few candidates of genuine worth offering genuine alternatives seem to be showing up on our ballots.[3]

Jake Tapper of ABC's *World News* commented that Colbert would be "the only presidential candidate who knows he looks ridiculous."[4]

In 2008, things looked like they might be different for Colbert than they had been for other comedians-turned-candidates. He was an actor and a comedian, but he also had a reputation for being a smart, savvy speaker with a keen finger on the pulse of the issues that were on the minds of American voters. He was a personality the American public responded to, in many cases more strongly than they did to genuine political candidates. Political analysts were not quite sure what to make of him, whether or not to take his bid for the White House seriously. Journalistic coverage in Colbert's home state of South Carolina expressed just that confusion. "Even political analysts are unsure if Colbert is serious or simply trying to gain attention. When asked to comment on how Colbert could affect the presidential race, CBS analyst Jeff Greenfield simply stated, 'This is going to be one for the books.'"[5] Afterward, Colbert himself insisted that at the time his bid had been real; he was taking his bid for the ballot seriously. "It wouldn't be a joke if it wasn't real," went his convoluted reasoning.[6]

At first Colbert asked to be placed on both the Republican and Democratic ballots in South Carolina—though he realized that this strategy could make him the only candidate who "can lose twice."[7] But the Republicans required a $35,000 fee to file for the state primary—a bit too rich for Colbert's blood. The Democrats, on the other hand, wanted just $2,500, which Colbert found affordable.

Journalists—*real* journalists, not those of the Stewart/Colbert variety—gave serious consideration to Colbert's impact on the election. Josh Green, writing for the *Atlantic,* consulted political experts on their opinions of a Colbert presidential run. His analysis was surprisingly very much in Colbert's favor as a Republican rather than Democratic candidate. Green wrote, "According to one presidential advisor, the South Carolina Republican electorate is 'monolithically white, much more male than female, and younger' than the Democratic electorate—all good news for Colbert. As a rule of thumb, younger voters tend to be more liberal than older voters." Colbert's home state, however, proves to be an atypical case: "In South Carolina, younger voters are more conservative than their counterparts elsewhere. Factor in 'Reaganiness,' and things could get interesting."[8]

Analysts began speculating on how far a genuine Colbert candidacy could realistically go, and what effect it might have on other candidates' chances. No one saw Colbert as a threat to Democratic front-runner Barack Obama or Republican hopeful John McCain. But with the parties' national conventions weeks away, there were still quite a few hats in the ring: Rudy Giuliani, Fred Thompson, and Mitt Romney, for example, among the Republicans; Chris Dodd and John Edwards among the Democrats. This was still serious company, and former comedian candidates had never been part of this top echelon. Green of the *Atlantic* believed Colbert was among these second-tier competitors. In fact, Green speculated, "if Colbert runs more than a 'front-porch' campaign—if he actually shows up and holds a few rallies—he'll suck up the media buzz any laggard needs to break through."[9]

Colbert focused his attention on getting his name included on the Democratic primary ballot. His goal, considering his egocentric character, was quite modest. "If, at the Democratic National Convention, somebody has to stand up and say, 'The proud state of South Carolina, the Palmetto State, the home of the greatest peaches and shrimp in the world, casts one vote for native son, Stephen Colbert,' I'd say I won."[10] For a while it looked as if a Colbert delegate at the convention might become a reality. Rather than compare Colbert's run for the White House with Pat Paulsen's obviously mock candidacy, reputable newscasters speculated on how many of South Carolina's votes he might sweep. A Public Opinion Strategies poll conducted in October 2007 saw Colbert carrying 2.3 percent of the Democratic vote—ahead of real candidates like Bill Richardson and Dennis Kucinich, and just trailing Joe Biden. A Rasmussen poll the following week indicated that, if the final Democratic race came down to Hilary Clinton, Rudy Giuliani, and Stephen Colbert, Colbert would hold his own nicely. *Editor and Publisher* predicted, "If he keeps gaining over 10% a week, Colbert should be leading the field before November is out."[11]

Unlike any comedian candidate before him, Colbert, along with Obama and McCain, was invited for an interview on the venerable news program *Meet the Press*. On October 21, 2007, Colbert was clearly in character as he chatted with host Tim Russert, but neither man was ready to acknowledge that the interview was a sham. When Russert asked what had prompted Colbert to toss his hat into the ring, Colbert replied, "I'm doing it, Tim, because I think our country is facing unprecedented challenges in the future. And I think that the junctures that we face are both critical and unforeseen, and the real challenge is how we will respond to these junctures, be they unprecedented or unforeseen, or, God help us, critical."[12] It was pure satire, politics by buzzword.

Colbert had a following. Colbert Nation had sprung up with little or no encouragement from him, and it wielded power, evidenced by the infamous Hungarian bridge naming. The social networking website Facebook also got involved. "Facebook.com, which doesn't claim to be anything more than a way to keep friends updated on your life, has a way of spreading political news and information. People share links with one another, comment on news stories, and join groups to show their political affiliations. Not surprisingly, the group supporting Stephen Colbert for President became one of the largest groups in the history of the Web site."[13] Acknowledging the popularity of Comedy Central in general, and Colbert and Stewart in particular, with the just-turned-18 crowd—a group about to vote in a presidential election for the first time in their lives, one journalist commented, "I can't point to anything other than truthiness, but I believe the 'drunken college student' demographic is being overlooked."[14]

Like fellow presidential wannabes Giulini and Romney, Colbert finally pulled out of the race on November 5, 2007. The executive council of South Carolina's Democratic Party chose not to include him on its primary ballot. Of course, he had never really been a viable candidate—although, considering the career paths of former actors Ronald Reagan and Arnold Schwarzenegger, Hollywood and Washington (or at least a governor's mansion) were not that far apart. According to Colbert, for some people involved with *The Colbert Report*, the decision was a relief. "The network was worried, and lawyers were worried, and I said 'Guys, they're never going to let me do it, so don't worry about it.' And sure enough, it only lasted 13 days. 13 days after I started, it was over. And then we're done. And I said Okay, everybody can climb down out of their tree now. I told ya."[15]

Nevertheless, Colbert and his host of fans and followers had made a significant point. A sizable portion of the American public was unhappy with politics as they had known it for years. The White House was far too full of the truthiness Colbert so glibly parodied on *The Colbert Report*. Voters were ready for a change. On his show, Colbert verbally threw his support to his character's party of choice, the Republicans, led by McCain. (Meanwhile, Jon Stewart, ever the liberal, tossed plenty of kudos to Obama.)

When Obama emerged the victor in November 2008, Colbert ranted and raved. But in the twisted way of Comedy Central's paired news/editorial shows, Obama's win proved the point Colbert had been illustrating through his own weird and wonderful bid for the White House. America *was* ready for a change, and its discontented masses had spoken by way of the voting booth.

And in alternate universes, hopes have not been dashed for a President Colbert. An interactive website launched in early 2008, just as the presidential race was beginning to heat up, was created by a team including Tarleton Gillespie of Cornell University. Called WikiCandidate, it worked much like the online encyclopedia Wikipedia in that users could alter its information. But unlike Wikipedia, the information on WikiCandidate was intended to be changed and even erased. The concept was that users could log in and create an ideal presidential candidate—everything from his (or her) biography, to his/her views on the issues. The connection with Colbert? The baseline WikiCandidate was patterned after him.

Marvel Comics, too, paid tribute to presidential hopeful Colbert. After appearing as a guest on *The Colbert Report*, Marvel's editor in chief Joe Quesada began peppering his comic books' pages with "Colbert for President" posters. In issue number 573 of *The Amazing Spiderman*, which appeared in November 2008, Spidey himself tries to cheer up Colbert as his bid for the White House seems to be slipping from his grasp. Can a superhero save him?

Meanwhile, in the DreamWorks animated film *Monsters vs. Aliens*, released in March 2009, President Hathaway is voiced by none other than Colbert, in charge of the country at last.

The Colbert candidacy lasted less than two weeks. Its end could not have come at a more propitious time. On November 5, 2007, the Writers Guild of America went on strike. All entertainment media—television, movies—involve teams of writers. When the new contract came up, negotiations stalled over issues like payment for DVD versions of programs, and what to do about Internet rebroadcasts. For weeks, there was no production of new television shows, *The Daily Show* and *The Colbert Report* included. Their stars might be the most visible aspects of both programs, but in reality there are many people involved in creating comedy like that. In early January, both shows came back on the air with no words in the teleprompters. Stewart and Colbert relied on their comedic backgrounds—stand-up and improv—to cobble together a ghost of their regular shows. The strike came to an end on February 12, 2008.

NOTES

1. "U. South Carolina Students Discuss Colbert's Presidential Bid." *Daily Gamecock* [Columbia, SC]. 19 Oct. 2007. *iCONN Custom Newspapers—U.S. Newspapers*. Web. 23 July 2010.

2. Staff, E. and P. "Stephen Colbert Appears on 'Meet the Press' to Discuss Race for President." *Editor & Publisher* (2007). *General OneFile*. Web. 23 July 2010.

3. Kurtz, Howard. "This Cracks Me Up." *Washingtonpost.com*. 23 Oct. 2007. *General OneFile*. Web. 23 July 2010.

4. Kurtz.

5. "U. South Carolina Students Discuss Colbert's Presidential Bid." *Daily Gamecock* [Columbia, SC]. 19 Oct. 2007. *iCONN Custom Newspapers—U.S. Newspapers*. Web. 23 July 2010.

6. Ferguson, D. B. "Exclusive Interview: Rev. Sir Dr. Stephen T. Colbert, D.F.A." *No Fact Zone*. 17 May 2011. Web. 23 July 2011. <http://www.nofactzone.net/2011/05/21/exclusive-interview-rev-sir-dr-stephen-t-colbert-d-f-a/>.

7. "U. South Carolina students."

8. Kurtz.

9. Kurtz.

10. Staff, E. and P. "Stephen Colbert Appears on 'Meet the Press."

11. Mitchell, Greg. "Obama Owes It All To—Stephen Colbert!" *Editor & Publisher*. (2008). *General OneFile*. Web. 28 July 2011.

12. Staff, E. and P. "Stephen Colbert Appears on 'Meet the Press."

13. Seitz, Jonathan. "It's an Online World for Young People and Political News." *Nieman Reports* 62.2 (2008): 10+. *General OneFile*. Web. 23 July 2010.

14. Kurtz.

15. Ferguson.

Chapter 10

TAKING THE SHOW ON THE ROAD

The most controversial and divisive aspect of the George W. Bush administration had been the war in the Middle East. President Barack Obama inherited it. Even if he wanted to end the conflict, it would take time. But in the meantime, people who were against the war still supported the thousands of American servicemen who had spent years fighting and dying in the desert.

Both Jon Stewart and Stephen Colbert had covered the wars in Iraq and Afghanistan in their own fashion. One of *The Daily Show*'s longest-running regular news segments was called "Mess o' Potamia." On his show, Colbert, in character as a staunch Bush supporter, blanched at any insinuation that the conflict was a mistake. But Colbert the person was aware of the sacrifice enlisted men and women were making thousands of miles from home. Colbert's show was popular with young people in the military both overseas and in the States. He had visited the National Naval Medical Center in Bethesda, Maryland, to cheer the injured. Since 2006, he had been doing a shout out to acknowledge service members who sent him flags. "I was loving that we were making these guys laugh in these terrible conditions," Colbert said.[1] Proceeds from his red plastic WristStrong bracelets went toward the Yellow

Ribbon Fund for injured veterans, and Colbert supported educational projects that benefitted soldiers' children through his involvement with an educational charity called DonorsChoose.

In his days as a fake correspondent on *The Daily Show*, he had frequently appeared in front of a television's infamous green screen, dressed in khaki fatigues, against an apparent background of a desert, or a bombed-out Middle Eastern village like Fallujah, claiming that he was a journalist embedded in a life-threatening military maneuver when in reality he was safe and comfortable in a studio. In 2009, the green screen came down. Colbert was going to Iraq for real.

On August 14, 2008, the guest on *The Colbert Report* was Marine Colonel Bing West. Colbert and West were discussing West's book, *The Strongest Tribe*. Suddenly, during a commercial break but still in front of a studio audience, West asked, "If General Petraeus invited you to come do your show in Iraq, would you do it?"[2] Colbert's response was polite but noncommittal: tempting as the offer was, any show is bigger than its star, and the decision was not altogether his to make. But it was too exciting an opportunity to pass up. And more than a hundred people, from all over the United States, some from other countries, had been stunned witnesses to that extemporaneous offer.

Part of the dilemma involved the character of the show itself. So much of Colbert's humor involves lampooning his subject. And, as he and his audience had seen at the 2006 White House Correspondents' Dinner, that sort of humor could backfire all too easily. Colbert had no desire to insult the troops. Yet they would expect no less than for him to appear in character, and that character had a way of being abrasive.

The answer came from an unanticipated situation. As economic woes filled newspaper and online news service headlines, the conflicts in Iraq and Afghanistan fell between the cracks. And Colbert had his avenue for humor, thanks to good old truthiness and wikiality. A person as in tune with gut feelings as Colbert the character would naturally reason that, if the war in the Middle East was no longer in the spotlight, it must have ended while he wasn't looking! As Colbert mused in a stint as guest editor for *Newsweek*, "I know what you're thinking: 'Isn't the Iraq War over?' That's what I thought, too. I hadn't seen it in the media for a while, and when I don't see something, I assume it's vanished forever, like in that terrifying game peekaboo. We stopped seeing much coverage of the Iraq War back in September when the economy tanked, and I just figured the insurgents were wiped out because they were heavily invested in Lehman Brothers."[3] With that mind-set, Colbert could visit the troops in Iraq and wonder, in character, what they were still doing there. Meanwhile, Colbert the actual person would be showing them that they had not been forgotten.

Since he would be spending a week on a military base in Iraq, Colbert sensed a perfect comedic opportunity. He enrolled himself to undergo basic training at Fort Jackson in his home state of South Carolina. There, Sergeant 1st Class Demetrius Chantz put Colbert through his paces: running, doing push-ups and sit-ups, climbing, tripping over obstacles in an attempt to negotiate a cross-country course, rappelling. A camera crew, of course, followed Colbert's embarrassing progress through the 10 hours of training. For Colbert, who is afraid of heights, the hardest part of the exercise involved climbing a tower, attaching himself to a rope, and easing his terrified self down. Throughout his training, he sang. He cracked jokes. And, finally, just once, he got Chantz, the epitome of a loud, direct, and stone-faced drill sergeant, to smile—by shushing him.[4]

Logistics made it impossible for Colbert to bring his entire crew of writers and camera- and soundmen with him to Iraq; only 30, about a third of the full contingent, climbed onto the commercial flight to Kuwait, the first leg of the journey. The rest of the trip, to the Baghdad International Airport, would be on a military C17 Globemaster. Colbert was encouraged by the South Carolina insignia serendipitously displayed on the plane's tailfin.

Colbert spent a week among the troops in Iraq. He was based at Camp Victory in Baghdad, just a few miles from the airport. A stage was set up in one of Saddam Hussein's decadently decorated former palaces. And there, Colbert taped four episodes of The Colbert Report just as he would any other week. But this was not an ordinary week. This was the week of Operation Iraqi Stephen: Going Commando. And it would be an historic event; never before had the U.S.O. "filmed, edited, and broadcast" a "nonnews show . . . from a combat zone."[5] Colbert's first words to his audience? "By the power vested in me by basic cable, I officially declare we have won the Iraq war!"[6]

Gone was Colbert's chic dark Brooks Brothers suit. For these shows, the designers had created a pseudo-military camouflage number, complemented by a stylish khaki shirt and tie. It was a far cry from the multipocketed safari vests he'd worn in front of the green screen as one of Jon Stewart's embedded war correspondents. And Colbert's dark waves of hair? By order of President Barack Obama ("General, as the Commander-in-Chief, I hereby order you to shave that man's head," Obama intoned via video), a cringing Colbert submitted to the razor, onstage, wielded by none other than General Raymond T. Odierno, who had replaced General Petraeus.[7]

On the base, Colbert had a hard time following military rules, and it had nothing to do with his comic character. In the New York studio, he is used to being everywhere at once, trotting off to wherever he happens to be needed. The army did not want any accidents while Colbert was on base, so he was always accompanied by a security guard—at least, theoretically. In his first days in Baghdad, however, he would be walking obediently alongside his handler, and would suddenly veer off to talk to someone, shake a few hands (Colbert shook an average of

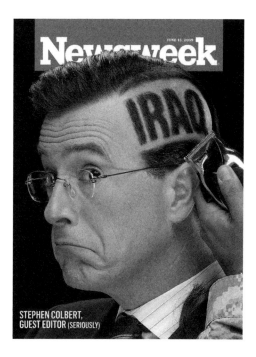

Stephen takes a close shave for the troops in Iraq. (PRNews-Foto/NEWSWEEK)

800 hands in two hours and, as a result, developed such severe tendon-itis that he had trouble holding a fork)[8] or take care of a bit of business. Repeatedly, he and his guards lost track of one another. The men and women Colbert was greeting and performing for loved the energetic, funny celebrity in their midst, but the army was growing frustrated with their visiting star. Finally, Morale, Welfare, and Recreation Officer Lieutenant Lisa Turner turned him over to a fellow South Carolinian, Navy Senior Chief Petty Officer Tony Rizi, with the strict order, "You are not to go anywhere without him, sir. If you do not take him with you, he is in trouble—with me. Do you want to get him in trouble?" Ex-cept for trips to the bathroom (when Rizi stood by the door and waited patiently), for the next five days the two men were inseparable. Since so many of his writers had been left back in New York, Colbert found himself using Rizi as a sounding board, editor, and critic for some of his military-themed jokes.[9]

During his sojourn in Iraq, Colbert had a second job to do. He was serving as guest editor for a special edition of *Newsweek* magazine, which hit the newsstands on June 5, 2009, just a few days before the Iraq shows aired. He took part of his job seriously, as Colbert the real person: many of the articles he selected for the magazine that week involved the military at home and abroad and their families. Other portions of the job were taken over by Colbert the character—the page of letters to the editor, for instance. There, Colbert included all the ultra-conservative letters he had sent to *Newsweek* between 1933 (from "Heaven's Waiting Room"[10]) and 2009 but for some odd reason the magazine had seen fit not to print.

The cover of that issue of *Newsweek* featured a picture of Colbert in profile, the word "Iraq" shaved into the side of his head. At Camp Victory, when he opened an urgent email in the middle of the night and saw that cover, Colbert was fuming; it was not what he and *Newsweek* had agreed on. There were supposed to be words below the picture, ques-tioning whether Americans had forgotten about the war—and those words were gone. Colbert was not sure what message readers would glean from the uncaptioned picture—so, in spite of the late hour, he tracked down some soldiers in a nearby mess hall to get their opinions. After they studied the image for a while, one young man offered, "It means Iraq is on your mind, and it should be on our minds too."[11] With high fives all around, Colbert thanked the soldiers for helping create his issue of *Newsweek*.

Colbert the character is always insanely patriotic. But Colbert the real person came home from his experience in Iraq with a new degree of patriotism, too—and it was not a side effect he had anticipated. Despite having family members who had joined the military, Colbert had grown up with a sense that there was *us*, ordinary people, and *them*, the armed forces, and that one group was somehow inherently different from the other. He also acknowledges that there is still a negative connotation to being in the military, which he blames on the Vietnam War and the 1970s antiwar movement.

His week in Baghdad, living on a military base, spending every hour of every day in the company of young men and women prepared to give their lives for America and all it stands for, opened his eyes. "There was just a sense of connection and gratitude to those people. My daughter called, or I called my daughter from Baghdad, and she goes what's it like, daddy? And I said, well, honey, you know, however you feel about the war, when my show started this was the worst place on earth in 2005. And these young men and women have worked hard to make it someplace that might, you know, be a functioning democracy someday. And you cannot help but feel proud for your nation in ways that I never have before."[12]

NOTES

1. Hymel, Kevin M. "Salute to Servicemembers: Comedian Stephen Colbert Inspires Troops at Home and Abroad." *Soldiers Magazine* 66.2 (2011): 16+. *General OneFile*. Web. 6 Mar. 2011.

2. Hymel.

3. Colbert, Stephen T. "Why I Took This Crummy Job—Newsweek." *Newsweek—National News, World News, Business, Health, Technology, Entertainment, and More—Newsweek*. Web. 21 July 2011. <http://www.newsweek.com/2009/06/05/why-i-took-this-crummy-job.html>.

4. Hymel.

5. Robertson, Campbell. "Stephen Colbert Takes His Show on the Road to Baghdad—NYTimes.com." *The New York Times—Breaking*

News, World News & Multimedia. 18 July 2011. Web. 18 July 2011.
<http://www.nytimes.com/2009/06/08/arts/television/08colb.html>.

6. Aamer, Madhani. "Live from Iraq: Comedian Colbert Delivers Laughs to American Troops." *USA Today.* n.d.: MAS Ultra—School Edition. EBSCO. Web. 16 Oct. 2011.

7. Lin, Joseph. "Colbert Takes The Show To Iraq—Top 10 Stephen Colbert Moments—Time." *Breaking News, Analysis, Politics, Blogs, News Photos, Video, Tech Reviews—TIME.com.* Web. 21 July 2011. <http://www.time.com/time/specials/packages/article/0,28804,2027834_2027833_2027946,00.html>.

8. Hymel.

9. Hymel.

10. Colbert, Stephen T. "A Note From Stephen Colbert—Newsweek." *Newsweek—National News, World News, Business, Health, Technology, Entertainment, and More—Newsweek.* Web. 21 July 2011. <http://www.newsweek.com/2009/06/05/a-note-from-stephen-colbert.html>.

11. Hymel.

12. "Stephen Colbert: In Good 'Company' On Broadway." *Fresh Air.* 14 June 2011. *General OneFile.* Web. 19 July 2011.

Chapter 11

SPINOFFS

In 2004, Jon Stewart had been hugely successful with a book spun off from *The Daily Show*. Titled *America: The Book (A Citizen's Guide to Democracy Inaction)* and written by Stewart and the same group of writers who created the television show, it was a parody of high school civics textbooks, complete with nude paper dolls of the nine Supreme Court justices. In 2011, Stewart and company followed up *America: The Book* with *Earth: The Book (A Visitor's Guide to the Human Race)*. Despite the character's "healthy skepticism about the printed word,"[1] it was inevitable that Colbert would hit the bestseller lists, too.

The fall of 2007 saw the publication of *I Am America (And So Can You!)*, written by Colbert and his staff of writers. It's a combination biography/manifesto of the character, "a Constitution for the Colbert Nation."[2] Colbert himself also narrated the audiobook version.

The book is an extension of the television show, as Colbert admits in his preface. "When the cameras go off, I'm still talking. And right now all that opinion is going to waste, like seed on barren ground. Well no more. It's time to impregnate this country with my mind."[3] "It turns out it takes more than thirty minutes a night to fix everything that's destroying America, and that's where this book comes in. It's not just some collection of reasoned arguments supported by facts. That's the coward's way out. This book is Truth. My Truth."[4] Interviewed by *USA Today*, Colbert (in character) elaborated on his agenda behind writing the book: "America is under attack by the media, by the homosexual agenda, and a culture of sexual promiscuity. This is an attempt to fight back by reminding us of when America was greatest and is giving us a blueprint to recapture it. And stories from my own life also, to illuminate how other people should live. I'm not saying that people should be just like me, but as close to me as possible wouldn't hurt."[5]

In the next 200-odd pages, Colbert (the character) offers his truth on his own life (which is quite different from the real Colbert's background: fake Colbert grew up with a mom and dad in the house, and attended Dartmouth, not Northwestern), politics, sex, immigration, religion. Like Stewart's titles, the book has indeed been a bestseller.

While *I Am America (and So Can You!)* is Colbert's best-known writing sample, he does have a few other publications under his belt. In 2003, Colbert got back together with his Second City/*Strangers with Candy* pals Amy Sedaris and Paul Dinello to create an illustrated novel: *Wigfield, the Can-Do Town (That Just May Not)*. For years, storytellers like Garrison Keillor and Jean Shepherd have milked the charms of small-town life for comic material. For their parody, the Colbert/Dinello/Sedaris team created a wannabe journalist who discovers a small town that, far from being the American dream, is closer to the epitome of the American nightmare: Wigfield. Beset with the sorts of problems that arise from having been built on nuclear waste (its oldest living residents are in their mid-40s), Wigfield is scheduled for destruction when a nearby dam comes down, unless its psychopathically wacky residents can convince the government their little town is legitimate and deserves to survive. The book is full of photographs by Todd Oldham, portraying Wigfield's denizens (Colbert, Dinello, and Sedaris in an assortment of costumes and makeup) and major points of interest (primarily strip clubs). Resplendent in drag (complete with thong), Colbert appears as, among other characters, Raven, a buxom exotic dancer. In its review, *Publishers Weekly* called *Wigfield* "one of those rare works of satire that combine creative form, uproariously funny text, and a painfully sharp underpinning of social criticism." In

Booklist, Carol Haggas added that the "scathing, silly, sardonic satire is as caustic as the toxic dump on which Wigfield lies" and is "written with the raw edginess one would expect from Second City alums and collaborators."[6] The trio of authors got together for the audiobook recording of *Wigfield* and occasionally took the show on the road to perform mini-play versions at various book signings around the country.

In 2005, not long after the debut of *The Colbert Report*, in one episode Colbert included a promotion for his self-published novel, *Stephen Colbert's Alpha Squad 7: Lady Nocturne: A Tek Jansen Adventure*. Discussion of the nearly 2,000-page science fiction book became a recurring feature on the show for a while, as Colbert tried to attract a publisher. Then the intrepid Tek (sporting an exaggeration of Colbert's own neatly coifed forelock of dark hair) began to appear on the show as a cartoon hero with Colbert's voice, saving the world, and especially its lovely ladies, from dastardly deeds and certain destruction. The animations even had a catchy theme song, extolling "super awesome spectacular ultra-spy" Tek, "sometimes loving, then killing the aliens."[7]

Eventually a team of writers picked up on the concept and created a comic book series featuring Tek Jansen and his trusty sidekick, a space dolphin. Publication by Oni Press began in 2007. The writers tapped to craft stories for the hero, based on the Colbert character but set in a sci-fi future full of evil aliens, were seasoned comic book pros John Layman and Tom Peyer. Both had worked extensively for Marvel and DC Comics, and both were fans of *The Colbert Report*. Their artist for the project is fellow Colbert fan Scott Chantler. While *The Report*'s writing staff has stayed out of the production of the comic books, Colbert himself remains involved. For instance, at first Chantler drew his frames in a style reminiscent of the J. J. Sedelmaier cartoons used on *The Colbert Report*. (Earlier, Sedelmaier had worked with Colbert on the "Ambiguously Gay Duo" animations.) Colbert wanted something edgier, something that took itself more seriously. Colbert's first comment to Chantler was "Tek doesn't smile." With that in mind, the artist has drawn Tek as "the most confident man in the universe . . . sort of 'Clint Eastwood in space.'"[8] In addition to the Layman/Peyer/Chantler collaborations, each issue of the Tek Jansen comics included a standalone short graphic story by Jim Massey, illustrated by Robbi Rodriguez.

In 2009, the five issues of the Tek Jansen saga were published in a hard-cover omnibus edition.

Colbert is one television celebrity who has not shied away from a subject often considered taboo: religion. TV hosts and correspondents seldom talk about their personal faiths. But both Stewart and Colbert have made religion a major part of who they are as television personalities. Stewart revels in his Jewishness, Colbert in his Catholicism. Both Colbert the person, and Colbert the character, are practicing Catholics and make no effort to hide the fact; on Ash Wednesdays Colbert appears on-air with a smudge of ashes on his forehead. Every year, right after Thanksgiving, he begins his usual rant against the commercialization and secularization of Christmas. One of his pet peeves is the prevalence of the expression "Happy Holidays" in place of "Merry Christmas." So it was inevitable that eventually Colbert would decide to do a Christmas special. It finally happened in time for the 2008 holiday season.

The special, called *A Colbert Christmas: The Greatest Gift of All*, debuted on Comedy Central on November 23, 2008. Colbert grew up watching 1970s-style holiday specials hosted by variety show personalities like Perry Como, Bing Crosby, and Andy Williams, where there was a loose story format punctuated by visits from guest stars who would perform a solo, or a duet with the host; the music would range from traditional holiday songs to specially composed numbers. Colbert followed this pattern for his special. The story line was that Colbert was stranded in a vacation cabin, fending off a godless killing machine of a bear, while his special was being recorded back in the studio. His musical guests included rocker Elvis Costello, country stars Willie Nelson and Toby Keith, smooth R&B singer John Legend, quirky indie songstress Feist, George Wendt as Santa Claus, the three Colbert kids in a very brief cameo appearance as themselves, and Jon Stewart—whose song tries to convince Colbert to forsake Christmas in favor of the latkes and dreidls of Hanukkah.

All but two of the seven songs were custom-written for the special. Adam Schlesinger was the composer of the sometimes catchy, sometimes take-off-on-a-carol tunes. No stranger to scoring, Schlesinger crafted music for films like *Music and Lyrics* and *That Thing You Do!* And the writer responsible for the wicked satire in the witty lyrics was himself no stranger to either Colbert or his guest star Stewart. David Javerbaum, a former *Jeopardy!* teen tournament finalist with a degree in musical theater from NYU, was *The Daily Show*'s executive producer at the time. He had been promoted to that position after working as the show's head writer—where he had gotten to know Colbert. (Javerbaum, incidentally, is the composer of the Tek Jansen theme song.) This was also not the first collaboration for the team of Schlesinger and Javerbaum. Their 2008 musical, *Cry-Baby*, had a short life on Broadway (68 performances), but that life was long enough to get the pair a Tony Award nomination for best score.[9]

Some of the *Colbert Christmas* songs required a bit of tweaking before making the show. Stewart, for instance, was not entirely happy with the hacky Hanukkah lyrics Javerbaum first gave him. If he was going to be persuaded to attempt singing at all, he wanted to make it much more real. Stewart and Colbert have been friends for a long time, and their relationship comes through in their scene together. So, says Javerbaum, "It was Jon's idea to make that song much more 'call and response' back and forth, to give them more of that opportunity."[10]

There are also quite a few songs that did not make it into the special—such as one written with the heavy metal band Metallica (*not* one of the potential musical guests) in mind. Based on the band's "Enter, Sandman," Javerbaum envisioned something entitled "Enter, Santa." The music would be classic, hardcore, head banging Metallica—but the lyrics would be "bright and innocent," full of talk about a jolly man "giving gifts to good girls and boys."[11]

Javerbaum's personal favorite from the songs he and Schlesinger penned for the special was the Costello number, "There Are Much Worse Things to Believe In." The song concludes the show on an introspective note: "It's not meant to be funny . . . it's also a little sad."[12] Sadly, it was nominated for but did not win an Emmy for Best Music and Lyrics.

Schlesinger and Javerbaum also did not win their Tony for *Cry-Baby*. But *A Colbert Christmas: The Greatest Gift of All* was nominated for the 2008 Grammy for Best Comedy Album—and this time *did* win. And this was in spite of the nasty head cold Colbert had come down with just in time for the recording of the album, a week before the special itself was taped. (Since "The Greatest Gift of All" in the show's title is, in cheesily tongue-in-cheek manner, a video recording of the show, the package needed to be ready ahead of time.) Colbert complains, "If you listen, you can hear that I have a hideous cold for the entire thing. Could not breathe at all. Absolutely a cartoonish cold, [with stuffed up accent] 'like I'd dalk like dis dee endire dime.'"[13]

All proceeds from the DVD of the show, and the iTunes downloads of its songs, were donated to Feeding America, a charity that operates food banks around the country. And the iTunes sales soared because, again, Colbert Nation mobilized for a worthy cause. For a while after their November 25 release, the songs from A *Colbert Christmas* topped the iTunes charts. Then, singer Kanye West, self-proclaimed "voice of this generation, of this decade,"[14] announced that he was releasing a new album, *808s and Heartbreak*, on iTunes on December 3. At that time, West's hyperbolic boast was not that far from credible; he *was* wildly popular, and his album would undoubtedly hit #1 immediately. So on *The Colbert Report*, in Operation Humble Kanye, Colbert asked his loyal fans to download A *Colbert Christmas* tunes by the thousands, thus bumping West's album out of the lead—and making Colbert the

A *Grammy for* A Colbert Christmas: The Greatest Gift of All. (*AP Photo/ Mark J. Terrill*)

real voice of this generation, of this decade. And, at least for a long enough time for Colbert to proclaim "Mission Accomplished," the efforts of Colbert Nation were successful. West's response? "Who the f*** is Stephen Colbert?"[15]

Though critical comments were mixed, Colbert himself had a great time doing the Christmas special.

> [I]t was a tremendous experience. It was incredibly joyful, I'm so lucky that those artists wanted to do it with me. I just wanted to do it, to begin with, it was so in keeping with my character, who was a Christmas originalist, and felt that Christmas was under attack, and it validated his idea of bears being dangerous, and also his idea that he had all these friends who would come over and sing with him. It captured a simpler time of an Andy Williams special. And on top of it, I got to win a Grammy. It adds to the legendarium of the character's own ego. It couldn't have been a more joyful experience.[16]

NOTES

1. Colbert, Stephen. *I Am America (And So Can You!)*. New York: Grand Central Pub., 2007, p. vii.

2. Colbert, p. ix.

3. Colbert, p. vii.

4. Colbert, p. viii.

5. Carol, Memmott. "Colbert Reports on why he is a Great American." *USA Today*. n.d.: MAS Ultra—School Edition. EBSCO. Web. 16 Oct. 2011.

6. "Amazon.com: Wigfield: The Can-Do Town That Just May Not (9780786868124): Amy Sedaris, Paul Dinello, Stephen Colbert, Todd Oldham: Books." *Amazon.com: Online Shopping for Electronics, Apparel, Computers, Books, DVDs & More*. Web. 21 Aug. 2011. <http://www.amazon.com/Wigfield-Can-Do-Town-That-Just/dp/product-description/0786868120/ref=dp_proddesc_0?ie=UTF8>.

7. "Tek Jansen Theme Song." *PoeTV*. Web. 21 Aug. 2011. <http://www.poetv.com/video.php?vid=11587>.

8. Ferguson, D. B. "Exclusive! Interview with Scott Chantler (Illustrator, 'Tek Jansen' Miniseries), Part 3." *No Fact Zone*. 5 Apr. 2007. Web. 21 Aug. 2011. <http://www.nofactzone.net/2007/04/05/exclusive-interview-with-scott-chantler-illustrator-tek-jansen-miniseries-part-3/>.

9. Carter, Bill. "A Send-Up of the Season, Some Sincerity Required." *New York Times*. 20 Nov. 2008: C3(L). *General OneFile*. Web. 24 July 2011.

10. Ferguson, D. B. "Six Degrees: Interview with 'Colbert Christmas' Lyricist David Javerbaum." *No Fact Zone*. 1 Dec. 2008. Web. 21 Aug. 2011. <http://www.nofactzone.net/2008/12/01/six-degrees-interview-with-colbert-christmas-lyricist-david-javerbaum/>.

11. Ferguson, "Six Degrees."

12. Ferguson, "Six Degrees."

13. Ferguson, D. B. "Exclusive Interview: Rev. Sir Dr. Stephen T. Colbert, D.F.A." *No Fact Zone*. 17 May 2011. Web. 23 July 2011. <http://www.nofactzone.net/2011/05/21/exclusive-interview-rev-sir-dr-stephen-t-colbert-d-f-a/>.

14. Dixon, Louise. "Kanye West: I'm The 'Voice of This Generation'" *Breaking News and Opinion on The Huffington Post*. Web. 24 July 2011. <http://www.huffingtonpost.com/2008/11/13/kanye-west-im-the-voice-o_n_143703.html>.

15. Kreps, Daniel. "Stephen Colbert Declares Victory in Operation Humble Kanye | Rolling Stone Music." *Rolling Stone | Music News, Reviews, Photos, Videos, Interviews and More*. Web. 24 July 2011. <http://www.rollingstone.com/music/news/stephen-colbert-declares-victory-in-operation-humble-kanye-20081205>.

16. Ferguson, "Rev. Sir Dr."

Chapter 12

RESTORING SANITY (AND/OR FEAR)

As the new 2010 television season got under way, Jon Stewart began promoting a rally to be held in Washington, D.C., in October: a rally to restore sanity. The concept was a reaction to a public gathering back in August, hosted by Fox television news anchor Glenn Beck: the Rally to Restore Honor. Fox News in general, and Beck in particular, hold conservative, Republican political views—the sort Colbert spoofs and Stewart attacks on their respective shows. Beck had drawn a crowd of about 87,000, predominantly right-wingers like himself. Not one to be outdone by either Beck or Stewart, Colbert quickly countered with a rally of his own, called the March to Keep Fear Alive, to be held in the same place and at the same time as Stewart's. For weeks, the two pseudo-hosts talked up their competing programs and agendas. Genuine news media started to take notice as it became clear that the rallies were not fabricated ratings ploys; they would really be happening, and people from across the country really were planning to attend. A correspondent with the journal *Canadian Business* even printed a sort of rally-specific travel guide to Washington, D.C., complete with information on buying swag, suggestions of places to stay and eat, advice on how to get to the capital (such as a free bus from New York sponsored by Arianna Huffington), and sightseeing highlights for those who could not get enough of Stewart/Colbert.[1]

Stewart and Colbert may be comedians, but both are very aware of the social, economic, and political problems in America, even as they make fun of those problems each evening. Their humor would not be as funny if it were not so bitingly perceptive and heartfelt. One thing both were noticing was that, more and more, political debate was turning into a dinner-table argument, won by the participant who could shout the loudest. "If we amplify everything, we hear nothing," explained Stewart.[2] The rally he was planning would be, not for the Silent Majority of the 1960s, but for "the Busy Majority . . . who think shouting is annoying, counterproductive, and terrible for your throat."[3] Stewart and Colbert— Colbert in particular—can get quite loud and vehement on their shows when the spirit moves them. But the very existence of their shows is predicated on the concept that, as Americans, we can look at the ironic aspects of even the most serious things we do, and laugh at ourselves. While people generally turn out for presidential elections, state and local elections tend to draw fewer voters, yet these elections can be important as well, and are often accompanied by the kind of genuine, homespun debate America was built on. Colbert in particular emphasizes the grassroots level of American politics on his show; the "Better Know a District" segment might not be something to take seriously, but it does place a focus on politics on a local rather than national level. The twin rallies were strategically scheduled to take place on October 30, the weekend before Election Day 2010, November 2. With a president firmly in place for a while longer, it promised to be a low participation point in the election cycle.

Stewart and Colbert knew more about what they did *not* want their rallies to turn into than what they expected them to actually look like. Stewart reminded potential participants that shouting and throwing things would not be tolerated—nor would nudity. *The Daily Show* also featured a video clip of a recent political rally held in North Korea—a parade in which thousands of people goose-stepped along the route in unblinking unison. That, too, was far from the comedians' vision.[4] As *Time* journalist James Poniewozik noted, "Stewart has called the rally a Million Moderate March, but he's really not an advocate for politically moderate views so much as he is for expressing views in a moderate tone of voice."[5] Paraphrasing the famous phrase from the 1976 movie *Network* (Colbert's favorite, by the way[6]), Poniewozik created a possible slogan for the rally: "We're mild as hell, and we're not going to take it anymore!"[7]

Inevitably, as the date of the dual rallies approached, Stewart and Colbert announced that they had agreed to combine their programs into a "Rally to Restore Sanity and/or Fear." (No doubt this had been the plan all along, but the two rivals playing against each other for weeks made for good comedic television moments.)

Saturday, October 30, dawned cool and, fortunately for the rally participants, sparkling clear in Washington, D.C. Buses from as far away as Indiana and Georgia disgorged throngs of people, who headed for the festivities at the National Mall. Actress and talk-show host Oprah Winfrey chartered an airplane to bring people to Washington. The size of the crowd could only be guessed at, as the National Parks Service did not actually count the people there for the rally. On the rally's Facebook.com page, more than 200,000 people had claimed that they expected to head out to Washington to see what Stewart and Colbert and guests had to say.[8] The day of the event, a Comedy Central executive joked that his estimate for actual attendance was upwards of 30 million. Colbert's inflated guess was six billion—the approximate population of the entire world. Stewart thought the number was closer to 10 million—but to get more accurate figures, he facetiously asked people to start a head count. The actual number was finally guesstimated at about 215,000.[9] Whatever the numbers, Washington, D.C., was in gridlock that morning, with uncharacteristic Saturday traffic jams rampant and hotel rooms fully booked.

There was a program and a plot of sorts to be followed. The overarching concept was that Stewart, portraying the voice of reason, would persuade his fearful colleague Colbert to recognize that sanity and reason could overcome fear. Recalling the emotional images of the 33 Chilean miners who had recently been rescued from a collapsed mine and brought to the surface one by one, Colbert emerged onto the stage from his fear bunker in a one-man capsule like the one used in the rescue. Unlike the somewhat more conservatively (yet patriotically) dressed Stewart, Colbert paraded his brand of patriotism in a flamboyant, superhero-style red, white, and blue jumpsuit. The pair delivered their message of political civility and bipartisanship with plenty of humor.

There were also guest appearances by a striking variety of performers, all part of the comedic mayhem. Singer Yusuf Islam, known in the 1960s and 1970s as Cat Stevens, began his song "Peace Train," only to be stopped after a few bars by Colbert, who announced that he did not choose to get on that train. So another musical guest—and musical train—appeared: Ozzy Osbourne with his "Crazy Train." Another musician who participated, returning from his appearance on *A Colbert Christmas*, was John Legend.

Around the perimeter of the gathering, a variety of left-wing groups representing causes ranging from abortion to legalized marijuana arranged their informational tables. While he did not formally support the rally, President Obama did authorize a bank of phones to be set up on the grounds to call potential voters and remind them of the election just a few days away. Conservatives in the form of Fox News were present, too, trying to assemble a counter-rally nearby.

Stephen Colbert and Jon Stewart co-host the Rally to Restore Fear and/or Sanity in Washington, D.C. (AP Photo/Carolyn Kaster)

Some came to the rally just to see what it was all about; others were fans of *The Daily Show* and/or *The Colbert Report*. Many got into the spirit of the day with costumes and placards, most combining the humorous with the insightful. "This Sign Is Heavy," read one woman's sandwich board. "The Only Thing We Have to Fear Is Rampant Hyperbole," announced a more serious sign. Wings, from angels' to giant bees', sprouted from human shoulders, and a person dressed as a banana wandered the grounds.[10]

In a country beset by a crippling recession, involved in a long-standing conflict thousands of miles away, and still recovering emotionally from a devastating attack nine years earlier, the light-hearted rally had a serious heart. As Stewart put it, "We live now in hard times. . . . Not end times."[11]

One disturbing impression did emerge from the day, and it was noted by both rally participants and newscasters. The biggest political rally of the decade had been organized, not by a politician or a political party, not by a genuine journalistic news program, but by a pair of television hosts who considered themselves actors and comedians, not activists. And the people who came to hear them often reported that they trusted Stewart and Colbert more than they trusted their own political leaders.

"The rally seemed to be channeling something deep," said an article in the *New York Times*,

> a craving to be heard and a frustration with the lack of leadership, less by President Obama than by a Democratic Party that many participants described as timid, fearful, and failing to stand up for what they see as the president's accomplishments. "I'm proud of Obama, but the Democrats in Congress, they're just running for cover," said Ron Harris, a lawyer from Laguna Beach, Calif., who came to celebrate his 64th birthday. "They couldn't sell bread to a starving mother if God was standing next to them." Some in the crowd expressed regret that it was comedians, not politicians, who were able to channel their frustration. "We don't have any place to turn," said Michelle Sabol, 41, a jewelry designer from Pittsburgh. Mr. Stewart, she said, gave voice to her feeling of frustration and isolation. Four friends, dressed as giant tea bags in a

spoof of the Tea Party, said Mr. Stewart and Mr. Colbert were the only ones they felt expressed their point of view.[12]

Media as far away as Australia (where both *The Daily Show* and *The Colbert* Report are wildly popular) carried coverage of the rally, and echoed the sentiment that "as potent hybrids of hacks and harlequins, they [Stewart and Colbert] belong not in the realm of journalism but in some fascinating new fifth estate."[13]

It would not be long before a member of that new fifth estate would be visiting Washington, D.C., again, for a very different reason.

NOTES

1. Coholan, Kasey. "Rally to Restore Sanity: D.C." *Canadian Business* 83.18 (2010): 121. MAS Ultra—School Edition. EBSCO. Web. 16 Oct. 2011.

2. Schneider, Craig. "D.C. Rally Draws Crowds, Laughs: Comedians Keep Event Light—With Some Political Undertones. Stewart Said Goal was Also to Provide hope." *Atlanta Journal-Constitution* [Atlanta, GA]. 31 Oct. 2010: A2. *General OneFile*. Web. 6 Mar. 2011.

3. Poniewozik, James. "Can These Guys Be Serious?" *Time* 176.18 (2010): 91. MAS Ultra—School Edition. EBSCO. Web. 14 Oct. 2011.

4. "Laugh at Them All You Like, These Guys Are Serious About Civility in Politics." *Australian* [National, Australia]. 23 Oct. 2010: 7. *Academic OneFile*. Web. 6 Mar. 2011.

5. Poniewozik.

6. P., Ken. "IGN: 10 Questions: Stephen Colbert." *IGN Movies: Trailers, Movie Reviews, Pictures, Celebrities, and Interviews*. 25 June 2003. Web. 12 Oct. 2011. <http://movies.ign.com/articles/425/425845p1.html>.

7. Poniewozik.

8. Poniewozik.

9. "Stewart-Colbert Rally Pegged at 215,000." *Canadian Broadcasting Corporation* [CBC]. 1 Nov. 2010. *General OneFile*. Web. 19 July 2011.

10. Schneider.

11. Schneider.

12. Tavernise, Sabrina, and Brian Stelter. "At Washington Rally by Two Satirists, Thousands—Billions?—Respond." *New York Times*. 31 Oct. 2010: A24(L). *General OneFile*. Web. 6 Mar. 2011.

13. "Laugh . . ."

Chapter 13

COLBERT V. CONGRESS

Stephen Colbert was building a career out of claiming, "I am an expert on anything and everything,"[1] including politics. His bespectacled face and his character's opinionated, ultra-conservative views were readily recognized by the American public. And sometimes, inevitably, the line between Stephen Colbert the man and Stephen Colbert the character blurred. Politics might be something Colbert the real person might not be particularly interested in, but his character couldn't seem to stay out of the political limelight.

On his show Colbert had often made jokes about illegal immigrants—especially the ones that gardened and cooked and cleaned around his character's house. Then, on July 8, 2010, Colbert's guest for the evening was Arturo Rodriguez, head of the United Farm Workers. Rodriguez mentioned his initiative called Take Our Jobs, in which ordinary Americans perform the chores of migrant farm workers for one day to experience firsthand how difficult those jobs can be and how essential the laborers who do them are. To date, Rodriguez said, only three people had signed up for the experience. Reaching across the table for a handshake, Colbert agreed to be the fourth.

Rodriguez may not have understood entirely that the man who had just agreed to support his cause was playing a character. And he probably did not expect Colbert to arrive on Hurley Farm in upstate New York with a camera crew in tow, determined to film a show segment. Colbert did spend a day in the fields with migrant workers, but it was Colbert the character: picking beans in the fields, asking his fellow farm workers outrageous questions, and generally shucking more corny humor for the cameras than real ears of corn for the waiting crates.

Colbert was not the only nontraditional farm worker Rodriguez brought to the fields that day; he'd also invited Zoe Lofgren, Democratic congresswoman from California. Lofgren was working on legislation that would affect jobs in American agriculture.

Seated on hay bales in a cavernous barn, Colbert filmed an interview with Lofgren, which aired on *The Colbert Report* on September 22, 2010. Off camera—and in spite of the surreal on-camera questions she had endured from Colbert, such as whether she would bear his anchor baby (a derogatory term for a child born in the United States, and therefore an American citizen, to illegal immigrant parents)—Lofgren issued an invitation of her own. When she presented her new legislation, would Colbert be interested in testifying in Washington? She felt his views on immigration in general, and immigrant labor in particular, would be valuable. Initially Colbert's producer demurred. For once, even Colbert was not sure what purpose an appearance before Congress by his character would serve. But he was intrigued. He contacted Lofgren and made sure she understood that he would be testifying in character, something other Congressmen might not appreciate: "You know, they're not going to be happy that I do this because I'm going to do it in character. I'm going to have to do it in character. There's no reason for me to go. But my character really feels like he has something to say and I'll do my best to say something through the character."[2] Lofgren assured Colbert that, as the head of the House Judiciary Committee's Subcommittee on Immigration, she could guarantee that would be no problems. After all, it would not be the first time a celebrity had appeared before Congress as an expert witness. The bright red *Sesame Street* muppet Elmo had preceded Colbert into those hallowed halls when the puppet pleaded for funding for music education in schools in 2002.

And so, on the morning of September 24, 2010, Colbert arrived in Washington, D.C., to testify before Congress. Needless to say, it was a media frenzy, with press and photographers eager to snag a picture and a sound bite featuring the comedian. As the proceedings of the Subcommittee on Immigration, Citizenship, Refugees, Border Security, and International Law's Hearing on Protecting America's Harvest got under way, Lofgren described the needs of farm workers and the urgency for immigration, then acquainted her fellow Congress members with the people who would be offering their testimony, including Colbert. "I'm happy that the United Farm Workers helped introduce me to Mr. Colbert, who I'd not met before, so we could spend a day on a farm together. His actions are a good example of how using both levity and fame, a media figure can bring attention to a critically important issue for the good of the nation."[3]

The problems Colbert had envisioned began almost immediately, before he had had a chance to say a word. Representative John Conyers of Michigan suggested that Congress should get on with the business of making laws and Colbert should go on with his business of crafting a funny show—separately. When Colbert—and Congresswoman Lofgren—appeared confused about whether he was being denied permission to testify, Conyers clarified, "No, no. I'm not asking you not to talk. I'm asking you to leave the committee room completely and submit your [written] statement instead." Turning off his microphone and dropping out of character guise, Colbert said, "I'm here at the invitation of the chairwoman, and if she would like me to remove myself from the hearing room, I'm happy to do so. I am only here at her invitation."[4]

Up until that point, Colbert had been nervous. But the interchange with Conyers awakened the improvisational actor in him:

I was thinking oh, this is fascinating. I have engendered a fight that I did not mean to. But what's actually more fascinating is not that I'm in it, what's more fascinating is that I don't know what's going to happen next. And that's just, as a [sic] improviser, that's what I like more than anything else, not knowing what's going to happen.[5]

What happened next was that Conyers backed off.

The serious side of Stephen Colbert as he testifies before the House of Representatives on immigrants' rights. (AP Photo/Alex Brandon)

Each person testifying that day had about five minutes to present orally the information he or she had already submitted in writing. Colbert began respectfully, "Good morning. My name is Stephen Colbert, and I am an American citizen. It is an honor and a privilege to be here today." It took him little time to get to his satiric point:

> As we've heard this morning, America's farms are presently far too dependent on immigrant labor to pick our fruits and vegetables. Now, the obvious answer is for all of us to stop eating fruits and vegetables. And, if you look at the recent obesity statistics, you'll see that many Americans have already started. . . . Now, we all know there is a long tradition of great nations importing foreign workers to do their farm work. After all, it was the ancient Israelites who built the first food pyramids. But this is America. I don't want a tomato picked by a Mexican. I want it picked by an American, then sliced by a Guatemalan and served by a Venezuelan in a spa where a Chilean gives me a Brazilian, because my great-grandfather did not travel across 4,000 miles of the

Atlantic Ocean to see this country overrun by immigrants. He
did it because he killed a man back in Ireland. That's the rumor.
I don't know if that's true. I'd like to have that stricken from the
record.

He went on to cite his experience in the field:

I participated in the UFW's Take Our Jobs campaign, one of only
16 people in America to take up the challenge. Though that number may increase in the near future, as I understand many Democrats may be looking for work come November. Now, I'll admit I
started my workday with preconceived notions of migrant labor.
But after working with these men and women picking beans,
packing corn for hours on end, side by side in the unforgiving sun,
I have to say—and I do mean this sincerely—please don't make
me do this again. It is really, really hard. . . . . This brief experience
gave me some small understanding of why so few Americans are
clamoring to begin an exciting career as seasonal, migrant field
workers. So what's the answer? I'm a free-market guy. Normally, I
would leave this on the invisible hand of the market, but the invisible hand of the market has already moved over 84,000 acres of
production and over 22,000 farm jobs to Mexico and shut down
over a million acres of U.S. farmland due to lack of available labor
because, apparently, even the invisible hand doesn't want to pick
beans. Now, I'm not a fan of the government doing anything, but
I've got to ask why isn't the government doing anything? Maybe
this ag jobs bill would help. I don't know. Like most members of
Congress, I haven't read it. But . . . maybe we could offer more
visas to the immigrants who, let's face it, will probably be doing
these jobs anyway. And this improved legal status might allow
immigrants recourse if they're abused. And it just stands to reason
to me that if your co-worker can't be exploited, then you're less
likely to be exploited yourself. And that itself might improve pay
and working conditions on these farms and eventually, Americans may consider taking these jobs again. Or maybe that's crazy.
Maybe the easier answer is just to have scientists develop vege-
tables that pick themselves. The genetic engineers over at Fruit of

the Loom have made great strides in human-fruit hybrids. . . .
I thank you for your time. Again, it is an honor, a privilege, and
a responsibility to be here. I trust that, following my testimony,
both sides will work together on this issue in the best interests
of the American people as you always do. [Laughter.] I'm now
prepared to take your questions and/or pose for pictures with
the grandchildren. I yield the balance of my time. USA—number one.[6]

After Colbert's prepared testimony ended, things began to heat up.
Representative Lamar Smith of Texas—a Republican, a member of the
party Colbert the character staunchly supports and defends—launched
an attack on Colbert's authority and credibility, questioning whether
he even knew how many of the laborers he had worked alongside on
the upstate New York farm were illegal, whether their pay was fair. As
for the day's pay, Colbert quipped, in character, "I didn't do a good
enough job to get paid so I can't compare my salary to anyone. I was
actually asked to leave." When it came to credibility, he explained,
more seriously but with characteristically sarcastic bite, "I was invited
here today by [subcommittee chairwoman Rep. Zoe Lofgren (D-Calif.)]
because I was one of the 16 people who took the United Farm Workers up on the experience of having migrant farm work for a single day.
If there are some other members of the committee who did that, then
I have no purpose being here." Did he qualify as an expert witness? It
was a dangerous question for Colbert the character. "I believe one day
of me studying anything makes me an expert." Finally, another Republican came to his rescue. Judy Chu of California asked Colbert to justify
his interest in immigration. This time, the answer seemed to come from
the man and not the character.

I like talking about people who don't have any power. . . . It
seemed like one of the least powerful people in the United States
are migrant workers who come and do our work but don't have
any rights as a result. And yet we still invite them to come here
and at the same time ask them to leave. That's an interesting
contradiction to me. And whatever you do for the least of my

brothers—and these seem like the least of our brothers right now. . . . A lot of people are least brothers right now because the economy is so hard. I don't want to take anyone's hardship away from them or diminish anything like that. But migrant workers suffer and have no rights.[7]

Many members of Congress were neither amused nor impressed. Majority Leader Steny Hoyer said, "What he had to say, I think, was not the way it should have been said." Hoyer added that the stunt was "an embarrassment for Mr. Colbert more than the House."[8] On the other hand, Speaker Nancy Pelosi, who has professed to being a fan of the show but not necessarily of Colbert's off-show antics, thought it was great that a popular figure like Colbert "can bring attention to an important issue like immigration."[9] The viewing public's reaction to Colbert's appearance on Capitol Hill, too, was not entirely positive. While some bloggers praised his action, The *Boston Herald* accused him of "making a mockery of a House hearing" and quoted Professor Tobe Berkovitz of Boston University, who stated that it was a "sad commentary on our political system when the Congress feels compelled to stoop to the lowest common denominator on important public issues."[10]

And how did Representative Conyers feel about Colbert's speech afterwards? The two men met to enjoy an amiable talk as they listened to some jazz. Conyers actually sent Colbert a note thanking him for taking the time out of his busy schedule to appear before Congress, along with a copy of the transcript. The irony was too perfect for Colbert to pass up. He had the letter and transcript mounted and framed together—with Conyers request that Colbert "leave the committee room completely" highlighted.[11]

Now that he had had a taste of speaking in front of legislative bodies, once was not enough. With yet another presidential election looming in 2012 and no desire to reprise his ill-fated bid for the White House, Colbert needed to find another way to involve his character, and his show, in the political process. And so he began to investigate PACs—Political Action Committees.

It is very expensive for a candidate to mount and maintain a campaign for a political office, whether local, state, or national. So organizations put together PACs to raise funding for the campaign of the candidate of their choice. Some types of PACs target employees of certain corporations or members of certain unions or organizations; others solicit money from the general public. One of the most visible activities of a PAC can be seen in candidates' advertising campaigns.

PACs have been a staple of the American political system for decades, but they have been growing steadily in size and spending power, especially recently. A Supreme Court ruling in 2010 creating a new form of PAC, the SuperPac, which could obtain unlimited funding from just about anyone: corporations, unions, and individuals alike. As long as they are not directly affiliated with or working under the orders of their candidate, SuperPacs can also launch a negative campaign with a degree of viciousness much greater than previously allowed. And in many cases, these PACs do not need to disclose who their donors are. Thanks to SuperPacs, the 2012 political campaigns could get interesting.

Palin has a PAC. So does Arkansas governor Mike Huckabee— almost Colbert's running mate back in 2008. So Colbert decided to investigate whether he could start a PAC, too. On March 30, 2011, his guest on *The Colbert Report* was Trevor Potter, former chairman of the Federal Election Commission, who explained in simple language what PACs were all about, how they were formed, and how the money could be used. Colbert appeared entranced by the possibilities (especially the idea of hiring a private jet with PAC funds). Then, Potter said that Colbert could use PAC money to create advertisements for candidates. Colbert's eyes lit up. Did the candidate need to approve those ads? On the contrary: He or she definitely could not ask for a supporting ad, and should not even know the PAC was creating its ad! And could Colbert create his own SuperPac? With the right forms correctly filled out, no problem, according to Potter. And so, repeating nearly word-for-word a statement he had made on *The Colbert Report*'s debut, Colbert put the question out to his studio audience and viewers at home: "Do you want your voices heard in the form of my voice?"[12] And the answer was a resounding yes.

As a television personality whose program runs on a cable channel owned by Viacom Communications, however, Colbert wondered whether there might be further legal ramifications when it came to his proposed SuperPac. To err on the side of caution, on June 30, 2011, he returned to Washington, D.C., to appear in front of the Federal Election Commission (FEC), hoping for clarification.

Once again, the sort of meeting that usually drew few if any spectators was thronged with fans and press. This time, however, viewers were probably disappointed that, at least during the meeting itself, Colbert barely spoke, so it was hard to tell whether he was in character or not. When asked for more detail about the kinds of advertisements he wanted to create, or where he wanted them to run, Colbert admitted, "We don't know what we're going to do with the ads, where we would place them, because we don't have the PAC yet. You're right in surmising that. That's why I hope to get the PAC, so we can find out."[13] He was putting himself out there as an Everyman, learning about a piece of the political process unfamiliar to most Americans, then presenting them with his discoveries, successes, failures, and mistakes, on national television.

The FEC discussed and voted. And it was unanimous: Colbert could indeed have a SuperPac. The involvement of Viacom, however, was a sticking point on which the committee could not agree. They finally decided that disclosure rules about use of Viacom's money for Colbert's SuperPac's ads would need to be in effect. Rather than hiding the identities of his contributors, Colbert ran a ticker at the bottom of the screen, honoring his proud donors, on every show.

Outside the FEC offices, Colbert immediately began soliciting for money for his new baby: "I don't know about you, but I do not accept limits on my free speech. I don't know about you, but I do not accept the status quo . . . but I do accept Visa, MasterCard, and American Express."[14] He accepted cash, too, which fans stuffed into bags held by Colbert's staffers. If they wanted receipts, they got their hands stamped "like patrons at Chuck E. Cheese."[15]

The FEC members were very aware of the incongruity of what had just happened. The vice chairwoman of the commission, Caroline Hunter, "noted the unique mix of the seriousness of Colbert's request and the nature of Colbert's show as political parody." She was pleased with the hearing's outcome. It affirmed a television personality's right to present genuine, useful information in a comic fashion. But, it was hoped, the restrictions would also prevent a SuperPac's being "used by other folks in a way that might not be so funny." Chairwoman Cynthia Bauerly also appreciated the odd nature of the moment. "While Mr. Colbert's request may bring some levity to campaign finance issues, the questions and concerns before us today deserve serious attention."[16]

Crowing about his SuperPac on *The Colbert Report* the next day, Colbert promised that his funds would go towards spots that would look nothing like ordinary, run-of-the-mill political ads; he would be a champion of "irresponsible advertising."[17]

The first test of the power of the Colbert Nation SuperPac—and its first example of irresponsible advertising—came in August of 2011. Rick Perry, Republican Governor of Texas, had recently announced his intention to run for president in 2012. The state of Iowa was holding a straw poll to see how potential Republican candidates would perform. Perry's name was not on the ballot, but write-ins were permitted. So the Colbert Nation PAC funded two television advertisements encouraging voters to write in the name of their candidate of choice: Rick Parry (with an *a*, not an *e*). CBS and NBC affiliate stations ran the ads; ABC declined on the grounds they would confuse voters.[18] Minnesota's Michele Bachmann garnered the highest number of votes, followed by Ron Paul of Texas—both coming in with more than 4,000. Write-in candidate Rick Perry (with an *e*) trailed far behind, with 718. And officials were not quite sure what to do with the Colbert-inspired Rick Parry (with an *a*) write-ins—count them as votes for Perry, or for a mystery candidate with an almost identical name.[19]

Several months later, as the South Carolina primary approached, the SuperPac funded a political advertisement portraying Republican hopeful Mitt Romney as a serial killer. Around the same time, Colbert toyed with the idea of once again throwing his hat into the presidential ring in his native state. Since he could not both run for president *and* run a SuperPac, he turned over control of the PAC to Jon Stewart; subsequent episodes of both *The Daily Show* and *The Colbert Report* featured mock struggles for power between the two comedians.

Yes, the 2012 presidential promises to be interesting.

NOTES

1. Wolk, Josh. "Mock the Vote." *Entertainment Weekly*. 3 Oct. 2008: 34. *General OneFile*. Web. 23 July 2010.

2. "Stephen Colbert: In Good 'Company' On Broadway." *Fresh Air.* 14 June 2011. *General OneFile.* Web. 19 July 2011.

3. "Hearing of the Immigration, Citizenship, Refugees, Border Security, and International Law Subcommittee of the House Judiciary Committee Subject: Protecting America's Harvest Chaired by: Representative Zoe Lofgren (D-CA) Witnesses: Arturo Rodriguez, president, United Farm Workers; Phil Glaize, chairman, U.S. Apple Association; Carol Swain, professor, Vanderbilt University Law School; Stephen Colbert, . . ." *Congressional Hearing Transcript Database.* 24 Sept. 2010. *General OneFile.* Web. 6 Mar. 2011.

4. "Hearing."

5. "Stephen Colbert: In Good 'Company' On Broadway." *Fresh Air.* 14 June 2011. *General OneFile.* Web. 19 July 2011.

6. "Hearing."

7. De Moraes, Lisa. "Moraes on TV—Mr. Colbert Goes to Washington." *Blogs & Columns, Blog Directory—The Washington Post.* 24 Sept. 2010. Web. 22 July 2011. <http://voices.washingtonpost.com/tvblog/2010/09/mr-colbert-goes-to-washington.html>.

8. "Comedian Stephen Colbert testified before the House Judiciary Committee's subcommittee on immigration, at the invitation of Rep. Zoe Lofgren (D., Calif.)." *National Review.* 18 Oct. 2010: 8. *General OneFile.* Web. 22 July 2011.

9. Marcus, Ruth. "Ruth Marcus—Stephen Colbert Becomes Another Circus of Congress's Making." *The Washington Post: National, World & D.C. Area News and Headlines—The Washington Post.* Web. 22 July 2011.

10. Heslam, Jessica. "Colbert's Congress Visit Called 'Sad Commentary'." *Boston Herald.* 25 Sept. 2010: 6. *Student Edition.* Web. 22 July 2011.

11. "Stephen Colbert: In Good 'Company.' "

12. "Colbert PAC—Trevor Potter—The Colbert Report—2011-30-03—Video Clip | Comedy Central." *Colbert Nation | The Colbert Report | Comedy Central.* Web. 23 July 2011. <http://www.colbertnation.com/the-colbert-report-videos/379369/march-30-2011/colbert-pac—trevor-potter>.

13. "There's Nothing Funny About Colbert's SuperPAC." *All Things Considered.* 30 June 2011. *General OneFile.* Web. 23 July 2011.

14. "There's Nothing Funny."

15. Reinhard, Beth. "Stephen Colbert Brings Reality TV to the FEC." *Nationaljournal.com*. 30 June 2011. *General OneFile*. Web. 23 July 2011.

16. "FEC Approves Colbert SuperPAC, Debates Viacom Disclosure Requirements." *States News Service*. 30 June 2011. *General OneFile*. Web. 23 July 2011.

17. Reinhard.

18. Winkler, Jeff. "Stephen Colbert | Rick Parry | Ames Straw Poll." *The Daily Caller*. 13 Aug. 2011. Web. 22 Aug. 2011. <http://dailycaller.com/2011/08/13/colberts-ads-advocate-rick-parry-write-in-create-a-straw-poll-mess/>.

19. Winkler.

Chapter 14

HEY, HE CAN ACT!

While the character from *The Daily Show* and *The Colbert Report* has been hugely successful for Stephen Colbert, he has not had many opportunities to flex the dramatic muscles he developed at Northwestern. He has had small parts in a handful of comedy films: *The Love Guru* with Mike Myers in 2008; *Bewitched* with Will Ferrell, Nicole Kidman, and Carell in 2005. And he has provided voices for minor characters on such animated series as *The Simpsons*; *American Dad;*, *Harvey Birdman, Attorney at Law*; and *Crank Yankers*. One of his few straight non-comedic roles was on a 2004 episode of *Law and Order: Criminal Intent*, in which he played an apparently gentle, mild-mannered, mom-loving, law-breaking forger and murderer. Fewer people saw his performance in January 2011, in a benefit staged reading of Harold Pinter's abstract memory play *Old Times* at the Luna Stage in West Orange, New Jersey; playing his character's wife in the play was the real-life Mrs. Colbert, Evelyn.[1]

So when later in 2011 Colbert was offered an opportunity to play a role in the musical *Company*—by none other than the show's composer, Stephen Sondheim, himself!—it was a nerve-wracking, scary, no-brainer of a decision.

As with so many of Colbert's most interesting stories, it all began with the choice of guests for upcoming shows. As 2010 drew to a close, Colbert was reviewing the guest roster for the next few days—and there on the list, scheduled for December 14, was composer and lyricist Sondheim, creator or co-creator of such Broadway musicals as *A Funny Thing Happened on the Way to the Forum*, *West Side Story*, *Sunday in the Park with George*, and *Into the Woods*. Colbert was beside himself. Seldom does he *seem* in awe of his guests, whether they are presidential wannabes, rock stars, film heroes, or bestselling authors, although he has admitted otherwise. This time was different. "People don't know this about me, that I really like musical theater." Colbert may not have trod the boards for decades, but his dramatic roots were still in live theater, and because of his training he still considered himself an actor: "[P]eople don't perceive what I do as acting, but I still do." He especially loved the work of his upcoming guest, Sondheim. "So I did something I never do with my guests: I did research." Colbert also had to think very carefully about how he was going to approach this interview. Much as he admired Sondheim personally, he had to consider how Colbert the *character* would view the man and his musicals. Colbert the character, always the under-informed, opinionated idiot, often plays ignorant with his guests, or gets hostile to evoke a funny reaction. "[A]nd it was hard for me to do that with [Sondheim] because I care so much about . . . his work."[2]

The approach Colbert took in his interview paid homage, with humor. Far from being an ill-informed idiot unfamiliar with the Sondheim canon, Colbert the character comes across as a fan who has seen the shows and knows the lyrics intimately—though he may appear to misunderstand them occasionally. One of Sondheim's most famous lyrics is "Send in the Clowns," from the musical *A Little Night Music*. Repeatedly, the sad singer asks, "Where are the clowns?" Taking the song far more literally than Sondheim intended, Colbert and his writers put their heads together and wrote another verse to the song, comically answering the question. Colbert sang the new lyrics to the familiar tune on the show:

Where are the clowns? I booked them for eight.
Hold on, that's them on the phone, saying they're late.

Traffic was bad. The tunnel's a mess.

All 12 of them came in one car; they lost my address.

You just can't trust clowns. That's why they're called clowns.[3]

At the end of the interview, Colbert came close to an uncharacteristic break in his character's persona. Quoting a line from *Sunday in the Park with George*, he said, "I rarely fawn because I like to seem more important than my . . . guests. . . . I'm so happy you came here. You and me, bud, we're the loonies. Did you know that? I bet you didn't know that. Stephen Sondheim, thank you so much."[4]

Not long afterward, Colbert's agent received a telephone call from Lincoln Center in New York City. Would Colbert—the person, not the character—be interested in being part of an all-star cast being assembled for an upcoming production of the Sondheim musical *Company*? Even before discussing it with Colbert, the agent turned the offer down, and upon hearing about it Colbert agreed it was the right thing to do; his own show was keeping him sufficiently busy. But the issue was not yet closed. A higher power than Lincoln Center made Colbert an offer he couldn't refuse. A letter came in the mail, signed by Sondheim himself, asking Colbert to reconsider because "You have a perfect voice for musical theater." When Colbert shared the letter with his wife, she said, "Boy, you have to do this. No one, let alone Stephen Sondheim, is going to ask you to do Sondheim."[5]

Because the production would star working actors with busy schedules, the cast members did not actually get together in one place until opening night. This being the technologically advanced 21st century, rehearsals were done via Skype. At first the cast members assumed it would be a concert-type reading of the show, with the performers arrayed on stage in front of music stands, singing their lines. But as they found themselves blocking scenes and learning choreography, they realized they had gotten involved in a fully-staged production.

Colbert had performed opera with his high school choir. He had taken voice lessons at Northwestern, and still sings occasionally on his show or in guest appearances. Judging from his performance on *A Colbert Christmas*, he is quite capable of carrying a tune, and is definitely a better musician than Jon Stewart. But he was unprepared for the challenges of singing the music of Sondheim. "To sing Sondheim is a completely different beast . . . there is a complexity of the note changes, like where you're going next in the song in Sondheim that isn't necessarily what you expect to do if you are mostly a la-di-da kind of guy." So he began taking voice lessons, something he had not done since college, with a coach named Liz Caplan. Colbert compares his voice lessons to yoga, but a form of yoga that concentrates on unusual body parts, like the soft palate and the sinuses. They worked on "things like resonance and projection and relaxation and just breathing."[6] And gradually, Colbert's vocal production approached Broadway quality.

Colbert was hardly the biggest name in this new *Company* company. He was playing alongside such Broadway and television talents as Patti LuPone (the original Evita from the Andrew Lloyd Webber/ Tim Rice musical of the same name), Neil Patrick Harris (of the 1990s classic *Doogie Howser, M.D.* and, more recently, *How I Met Your Mother*), Jon Cryer (*Two and a Half Men*), Christina Hendricks (*Mad Men*), and Martha Plimpton (*Raising Hope*). They would be portraying an assortment of wealthy but not especially happy Manhattanites of the 1970s, 30-something couples and still-looking singles reflecting on the positive, negative, and especially ambiguous aspects of their respective life choices. Colbert plays Harry, a married man, whose big number, "Sorry-Grateful," an intensely emotional lyric about his relationship with his wife, is sung to a confirmed bachelor played by (of course) Harris.

The show, part of the New York Philharmonic's spring gala, opened at Lincoln Center's Avery Fisher Hall on April 7, 2011. And as soon as that first performance was over, Colbert scooted downtown about eleven blocks and taped the Thursday evening installment of *The Colbert Report. Company* played for another three sold-out performances that Friday and Saturday (after which Colbert did *not* need to hurry back to the studio), closing on April 9.

Since Colbert has been more public about his improvisational comedy background than his dramatic and musical training at Northwestern, critics were a bit stunned that the man known best for playing an ignorant, overbearing buffoon on Comedy Central could actually portray deep emotions, sing, and dance—and do physical comedy, too. *Company* was filmed live, and the movie was distributed to select theaters around the country for a limited engagement during June of 2011. At this time it does not appear to be available on DVD.

While *Company* took up so much of Colbert's time during the late winter and spring of 2011, not once did he—or, rather, his alter-ego—mention the show on *The Colbert Report*. Even when he loped onto the studio stage on April 7, fresh (but exhausted) from opening night, his character did not gloat or brag or say a word about having just done Sondheim in front of a sold-out audience. And it all had to do with the difference between Colbert the person, and Colbert, the character. The guy onstage at Lincoln Center was the person, the actor—*not* the character. And for this project, Colbert was keeping his two personae far apart from each other. "Not that I think that the things that my character mentions on the show get poisoned by the mention, but there is a level that people could . . . ascribe an insincerity to the things that I tout on the show. And I didn't want to ascribe any insincerity to trying to go do this thing at Lincoln Center and—because I knew that . . . I was dealing with somebody else's delicate product, and I didn't want to invest it with my character's ego because it would just flavor what I was doing in a way that I don't think would be useful to the production." Also, Colbert was a little insecure about doing live theater. "I had no idea whether I wanted anyone to know I was doing it, because I knew how hard it was going to be, and I was afraid I would suck."[7]

Critics and audiences agreed, at least for the most part, that suck he most certainly did not. "The first surprise was how wonderful a stage performer and serviceable a singer Stephen Colbert [is] . . . " says Jonathan Mandell in *The Faster Times*; he also praises bits of Colbert's stage business as "delectable."[8] "Colbert and Cryer in particular sing like first-time skaters skate," counters Nelson Pressley in *The Washington Post*—who nevertheless credits Colbert's "delectably" (again!) "tetchy" performance as contributing to a *Company* that "is probably as well-acted as this beloved 1970 Sondheim musical (about a single guy lost amid his married friends) has ever been."[9]

While he may not be giving up his 54th Street studio for the Great White Way any time in the near future, looking back on the experience, Colbert says, "Being in 'Company' was the most wonderful trouble I've ever been in."[10]

NOTES

1. S. W. "Reviews: Stephen & Evelyn Colbert Perform 'Old Times' at Luna Stage Benefit." *No Fact Zone*. 13 Jan. 2011. Web. 16 Oct. 2011. <http://www.nofactzone.net/2011/01/13/reviews-stephen-evelyn-colbert-perform-old-times-at-luna-stage-benefit/>.

2. "Stephen Colbert: In Good 'Company' On Broadway." *Fresh Air*. 14 June 2011. *General OneFile*. Web. 19 July 2011.

3. "Stephen Sondheim—The Colbert Report—2010-14-12—Video Clip | Comedy Central." *Colbert Nation | The Colbert Report | Comedy Central*. 14 Dec. 2010. Web. 22 Aug. 2011. <http://www.colbertnation.com/the-colbert-report-videos/368532/december-14-2010/stephen-sondheim>.

4. "Stephen Sondheim."

5. "Stephen Colbert: In Good 'Company.'"

6. "Stephen Colbert: In Good 'Company.'"

7. "Stephen Colbert: In Good 'Company.'"

8. Jonathan, Mandell. "Company Review. All-Star Sondheim Sublime. New York Theater." *The Faster Times*. 9 Apr. 2011. Web. 16 Oct. 2011. <http://www.thefastertimes.com/newyorktheater/2011/04/09/company-review-all-star-sondheim-sublime/>.

9. Pressley, Nelson. "Critic Review for Stephen Sondheim's Company on Washingtonpost.com." *The Washington Post: National, World & D.C. Area News and Headlines—The Washington Post*. 10 June 2011. Web. 16 Oct. 2011. <http://www.washingtonpost.com/gog/movies/stephen-sondheims-company,1208184/critic-review.html>.

10. "Stephen Colbert Sings in Sondheim Show." *The Post and Courier, Charleston SC—News, Sports, Entertainment*. 24 Apr. 2011. Web. 24 July 2011. <http://www.postandcourier.com/news/2011/apr/24/colbert-sings-in-sondheim-show/>.

Chapter 15

WHO'S THE MAN?

So, since the character known as Stephen Colbert is more often than not what the public sees, who is the *real* Stephen Colbert, and what is *he* like today?

The real Colbert lives on a cul-de-sac in Montclair, New Jersey. Montclair Township, about 12 miles from New York City and boasting an impressive view of the city's skyline, is also home to a number of other figures from the world of television and entertainment, including dancer Savion Glover and film director Steven Spielberg.

Besides Colbert, the Colbert family consists of wife Evelyn "Evie" McGee-Colbert, and their three children, Madeline ("Maddie") Peter, and John, plus the family dog. Evie has acted alongside her husband on television in his comedy shows, but she is not a comedian per se—and Colbert is glad for it. And, while his character is unswerving in his belief in his own decisions, the real Colbert relies heavily on Evie's wisdom. "Any major decision I make, I say, 'I'm going to talk to my wife about it.' I call her my 'breathtakingly levelheaded girl.' I'm not a dumb guy, but she's smart and very clearheaded about things. I approach things very emotionally, and she does not, strangely enough. If I need to know if what I'm writing about still appeals to humans, I'll show it to her. I married a human being. Thank God I didn't marry another comedian, or else I'd be doing terribly, terribly dark humor all the time. . . ."[1]

Maddie, Peter, and John Colbert have all made appearances on *The Daily Show* as well as on *A Colbert Christmas*. But they are far from a show business family. In fact, when the children were younger, Colbert told the *New York Times*, "I don't want my kids to perceive me as a performer. . . . I tell them I am a chiropodist. I think that's a chiropractor for feet." Colbert is the kind of dad who reads to the kids in the evening. He added, "I am big on hugging. We are very silly. We fall down for each other. We do pratfalls."[2] Colbert's professional life takes a back seat to the needs of his children. He has been known to agree to guest appearances on shows only if it doesn't conflict with his picking his son up from swim practice.[3]

Colbert's old friends are still part of his and his family's life. He has remained close to those fellow geeks he played Dungeons and Dragons with back in high school; two of them are godfathers to Peter and John. One of those former geeks, Chip Hill, helped Colbert build a

Stephen and his wife, Evelyn McGee-Colbert. (AP Photo/Kevin Wolf)

rowboat during one of the Colberts' two-week-long summer vacations in Charleston. They then started a tradition of using the boat to take their boys fishing. Hill appreciates how different Colbert is from many celebrities. "He obviously comes from a large family, and his own family is very, very important to him. . . . You know, the typical story is a guy gets famous and loses perspective on their life. He works very hard to stay grounded."[4] Colbert enjoys being out on the water; in the spring of 2011 he participated in a sailing race from South Carolina to Bermuda.

Of course as Colbert's popularity, and his children, grew, it was impossible to continue the ruse that dad was a chiropodist. Dad's job changed to being "professionally ridiculous."[5] But the Colbert kids were not raised in a home full of The Daily Show or The Colbert Report. In fact, growing up, they seldom saw either program. And, as with so much in Colbert's life, it was because he was not his alter-ego. As Colbert explained to Morley Safer in an interview on CBS's 60 Minutes, "I truck in insincerity. With a very straight face, I say things I don't believe. Kids can't understand irony or sarcasm, and I don't want them to perceive me as insincere."[6] Colbert elaborated on that statement with Tim Russert, the late host of Meet the Press, "I look like their dad and I sound like their dad pretty much, but I just say things I don't mean. A child is just not gonna know that's a character, and they're gonna think I don't mean it when I say that I'm proud of them, or I don't mean it when I say I love them. You know, I'm gonna tuck them into bed one night and I'll say, 'I love you, honey,' and they'll say, 'That's good, Dad, that's very dry.'" Fortunately, Colbert adds, because of his improvisational training he finds switching in and out of his character as easy as taking off a cap.[7]

The Colbert family goes to Mass every week. Colbert even teaches a children's Sunday school class (most certainly not in character). He is the catechist in charge of the seven year olds, who are preparing for their First Holy Communion.[8] "I would say that there would be plenty of Catholics in the world who would think of me as not that observant, but for the world I move in professionally, I seem monastic."[9] Nevertheless, traditions, including religious traditions, remain important to the Colbert family. Growing up, the previous generation of Colbert kids would process through their James Island home singing carols on

Christmas Eve, "and we still do it. My family is 50 people now—nieces and nephews and that sort of thing—and we process from the youngest to the oldest. The youngest puts the baby Jesus in the manger on Christmas Eve and we sing 'Silent Night.' It's very traditional."[10]

Besides his religion, another way the real Colbert stays grounded is through the charities he supports. Some he promotes through his character. For instance, on July 21, 2007, while he was running around the set in his standard pre-show audience pump-up, he took a nasty fall off the dais and landed heavily on his hands, actually asking afterward whether anyone in the studio was an osteopath.[11] For a month afterward Colbert sported a brace, finally appearing in a cast on the July 26 show. It turns out he actually broke his left wrist. Colbert devoted quite a bit of time during his shows of the next four weeks to various topics on orthopedic safety. And people did what people always do with a cast: they signed it. But when you're Colbert, those signers could include Nancy Pelosi, Bill O'Reilly, and New York mayor Michael Bloomberg. When the cast finally came off—removed by Colbert's Dr. Vizzone during the taping of the August 23 show—Colbert put it up for auction on ebay.com. It fetched $17,200. But after the cast disappeared, a plastic bracelet took its place. Taking inspiration from bicyclist Lance Armstrong's LiveStrong cancer awareness campaign with its yellow bracelets, Colbert (the character) was starting a campaign of his own: WristStrong. For a few days, members of the studio audience received the bracelets for free, with the instruction to give them to someone more famous. Then the bracelets were offered for sale on the Colbert Nation website for $5. Before long, WristStrong bracelets were seen on the arms of politicians (including President Obama), entertainers, and astronauts on the space station. All the money earned through WristStrong—$350,000 and still growing—was and is donated to the Yellow Ribbon Fund, which provides services to veterans and their families.

Colbert the person supports some charities his character does not mention quite as overtly on-air. Among those is DonorsChoose, on whose 14-member board of directors Colbert serves. Colbert was fortunate to have attended high-quality schools, and feels strongly about the benefits of education (in spite of what his character may say). DonorsChoose, a sort of online matchmaking site linking worthy classroom projects in need of funding with prospective donors, was founded by

Charles Best in 2000, and has since attracted heavy-hitting supporters including Bill Gates. Half in and half out of character, after a visit to Manhattan Bridges High School to promote a new DonorsChoose grant program, Colbert told the Associated Press, "As I endeavor to protect our children from bears, donorschoose.org is protecting public school kids from classrooms that lack the materials necessary to rigorously prepare them for college."[12] Colbert supports additional charities including First Book, Save the Children, Feeding America, and Autism Speaks.[13]

According to his college transcripts, Colbert has a Bachelor's degree from Northwestern. But he can call himself Dr. Colbert thanks to honorary degrees from Knox College (a 2006 honorary doctorate in fine arts) and his alma mater, Northwestern (2011). (He can also add the title Sir to his name, having been knighted by Queen Noor of Jordan in 2009.) Colbert gave commencement speeches at both schools, heavily in character but also in part the real guy. As he explained at Knox College, "I'm facing a little bit of a conundrum here. My name is Stephen Colbert, but I actually play someone on television named Stephen Colbert, who looks like me, and who talks like me, but who says things with a straight face he doesn't mean. And I'm not sure which one of us you invited to speak here today. So, with your indulgence, I'm just going to talk, and I'm going to let you figure it out." He went on to describe life after college as the ultimate improv experience: "Well, you are about to start the greatest improvisation of all. With no script. No idea what's going to happen, often with people and places you have never seen before. And you are not in control. So say 'yes.' And if you're lucky, you'll find people who will say 'yes' back."[14]

Colbert's 2011 address at Northwestern struck many of the same chords.

> Dreams can change. If we'd all stuck with our first dream, the world would be overrun with cowboys and princesses. Whatever your dream is right now, if you don't achieve it, you haven't failed, and you're not some loser, but just as importantly—and this is the part I may not get right and you may not listen to—if you do get your dream, you are not a winner. After I graduated from here, I moved down to Chicago and did improv. Nor there are very few rules to improvisation, but one of the things I was taught early

on is that you are not the most important person in the scene. Every body else is. And if they are the most important people in the scene, you will naturally pay attention to them and serve them, but the good news is you're in the scene, too. So hopefully to them you're the most important person, and they will serve you. No one is leading, you're all following the follower, serving the servant. You cannot win improv. And life is an improvisation. You have no idea what's going to happen next and you are mostly just making things up as you go along. And like improv, you cannot win your life.[15]

The multiple personalities of Colbert have sometimes had weirdly existential ramifications. For instance, on April 22, 2010, the musical guest on *The Colbert Report* was the virtual band Gorillaz. The group is a bit like a modern-day, high-tech version of the Monkees: while its music is provided by a group of talented musicians working behind the scenes, its front men are cartoons, animations created by comic book artist Jamie Hewlett. On the show, Colbert, in character, discovers that he will not be interviewing the cartoons, but rather Hewlett and composer/musician Damon Albarn, in the flesh. Brooks Brothers-clad Colbert blusters, "I booked the band! No, this is bulls***! No, f*** this, I'm not interviewing them! No! No! No!" and stomps off the stage. A moment later he is replaced by—himself, but in a soft-spoken persona who introduces himself as Steve COLE-bert (hard "t") and is casually dressed in a striped rugby shirt. He explains to Albarn and Hewlett, "Stephen left. He's the real host and he would only interview the real band. So they sent me." He looks around the soundstage with awestruck wonder. "Cool." Then he gets down to a kinder, gentler version of business. "Stephen left me some of his questions." Colbert peruses a note card, looks up at his guests mildly, and recites, softly, incongruously, almost apologetically, "The first one is, 'Who the f*** do you think you are?'" It's an Alice-through-the-Looking-Glass moment: made-up Colbert would only interview the made-up Gorillaz, so real Colbert must interview the real Gorillaz guys. The conversation gradually steers toward psychologist Carl Jung. Albarn tries to explain Gorillaz in terms of daimons—other manifestations of a self—and archetypes. Colbert takes the concept a step further: "There's a deep psychological underpinning to the fact that the band has a persona that is created for a persona, since all bands truly have a persona."[16] Savvy viewers realize that Colbert is talking about far more than a band with cartoon frontmen; he is referring to himself and his alter-ego, the character Stephen Colbert.

From Monday through Thursday, Colbert drives from Montclair to his office in Manhattan. He wears khakis and polo shirts; the Brooks Brothers suits do not go on until it is time to tape the evening's show. The shelves on the set of *The Colbert Report* are full of things that are important to the character. The things that are important to the man are reserved for the walls of the office. And the man who inhabits that office has not changed much since his high school D&D days, though now that he has connections he gets his decorative swag from some very different sources. There is, for instance, a pinball machine with a *Lord of the Rings* movie theme. A photograph of Viggo Mortensen, who played Aragorn in the films—etched in edible chocolate. Anduril, Aragorn's sword—the actual movie prop—presented to Colbert by Mortensen himself. A few personal items in the office are not *LOTR*-based. There is, for instance, one of Colbert's Emmy Awards from his *The Daily Show* days—but he never bothered to attach the plaque bearing his name. And, rather surprisingly for most visitors, there is a 1972 Richard Nixon presidential campaign poster in a place of honor on the wall. It is not meant to be satirical; this is one Republican president Colbert—the real Colbert—truly admires. "He was so liberal! Look at what he was running on. He started the EPA. He opened China. He gave 18-year-olds the vote. His issues were education, drugs, women, minorities, youth involvement, ending the draft, and improving the environment. John Kerry couldn't have run on this! What would I give for a Nixon?"[17]

The late Tim Russert once asked Colbert how he prepares for *The Colbert Report*. "I read a lot of newspapers and watch a lot of news," Colbert replied. Then he and the show's "twelve great writers . . . chop wood all day long. We show up exasperated or angry about something and we try to turn that into jokes six hours later."[18] One of Colbert's head writers, Richard Dahm, is glad his boss is Colbert the man and not Colbert the character. "There couldn't be a huger difference between the character Colbert and the real Colbert," says Dahm. "The real

Stephen is an amazing guy. The character Stephen—well, I wouldn't want to be working for him."[19]

When the evening's taping is done, Colbert drives the 40 minutes back home to Montclair. It gives him some much-needed time to unwind—not from being Colbert the character, but from "being a writer and executive producer and the star. Being a writer and executive producer and the star requires a great deal of my focus. Letting go and not being the boss is much harder [at the end of the day] than letting go of my character. . . . The network would happily—they don't want me tired; they don't want me running off the road—they'd happily send me home in a car. But I'd work the entire way home, and I need more than the 30 seconds from the car to the front door to become a dad and a husband again. So I drive home and I crank my tunes. And by the time I get there, I'm normal again."[20]

Both Colbert as an individual performer and the team responsible for creating The Daily Show and The Colbert Report have been nominated for a number of media honors, including the Emmy (for television production, primarily entertainment-oriented programming), the Peabody (for television production in a wider range of fields than the Emmy), the Television Critics Association Award, the Producers Guild of America Award, the Writers Guild of America Award (as in those guys and gals who went on strike in 2008), and the Satellite Award (outstanding achievement in film, television, or other media). In 2008, Colbert himself won a Satellite Award as outstanding performer. But, since the creation of The Daily Show and The Colbert Report represents such a group effort, it seems appropriate that most of the awards actually won honor the writing and production teams rather than just Colbert. (Stewart owns Busboy Productions; Colbert's company is called Spartina, after a type of swamp grass common in coastal South Carolina. Animated logos for both can be seen at the end of each Colbert Report.) In 2008 and 2010, Emmy Awards went to The Colbert Report team for outstanding writing, as did 2011's WGA Award. The show also won PGA awards in 2008, 2009, and 2010 for outstanding production. The writers of The Daily Show (including Colbert) won Emmy Awards in 2004, 2005, and 2006. Thanks to "Indecision 2000" and "Indecision 2004," the show's coverage of the presidential races (in which Colbert was extensively featured as a correspondent), The

Daily Show won two Peabody Awards for "distinguished achievement and meritorious public service by stations, networks, producing organizations and individuals." In 2007, Colbert, representing the team at *The Colbert Report*, added a Peabody of his own to his collection. In his acceptance speech, he compared his writers to an enema, because they were so good at "injecting themselves into a story and flushing out the truthiness."[21]

Colbert has played host to everyone from rock stars to congressmen, and he is the hero of Colbert Nation. But who are Colbert's own heroes?

First, there's his mom, Lorna Colbert. As he said in a 2011 interview, "she is 91, still loves life, and has reason to be bitter, and is not. And that is the greatest inspiration that you can take into anything you do. That every day is a choice. And she always makes the choice to love that we are here. And that is a gift that I can never repay."[22]

And of course there is his former boss and once and future friend, the man who gave him the chance to develop his character and take him places no fake journalist had ever been before, Jon Stewart. "I'm lucky to have him as a friend, and as a mentor," says Colbert.[23] One thing Colbert especially admires about Stewart is that, while both men frequently host authors on their shows, Stewart actually reads more of their books. "Jon is the fastest reader I've ever seen. . . . [H]e really reads those people's books,"[24] unlike Colbert. While the two men came from very different comedy backgrounds, it was Stewart who taught Colbert all he knows about producing, writing, and performing in a satirical news show. Colbert also admires how Stewart still seems to love every minute of what he is doing—despite the fact that he has been doing it for more than a decade: "he has never dropped it, after 12 years he's still, every day gives everything. And that's an inspiration to me, that he can stay so focused after all these years and really seem to enjoy himself." Meanwhile, just as in their days together on *The Daily Show*, they continue to bounce ideas off each other after-hours, helping each other keep their respective routines fresh and sharp.[25]

Stewart has plenty of respect for Colbert, too, especially for his intelligence—and, coming from a smart guy like Stewart, that is saying a lot. "He'd be comfortable not only in any discipline, but in any era," says Stewart. "If you transplanted him to the 1600s and suddenly he was involved in the medieval arts, or even dentistry, he would be fine. I consider him, oddly enough, like the Internet."[26] Stewart adds, "Stephen's brain has more folds than most people. I like to keep my brain shiny and smooth, but his is all foldy."[27]

So what comes next for Colbert? It's always hard to tell, because of his penchant for throwing his character into the midst of whatever is happening on the political (or entertainment, or *any*) scene. He has said that there is one straight dramatic role he would love to sink his teeth into: Richard Rich in Robert Bolt's *A Man for All Seasons*. The play is about Sir Thomas More, who was beheaded for opposing King Henry VIII's divorce from Catherine of Aragon so he could marry Anne Boleyn; Rich, once More's friend, ends up betraying him.[28] A rabid Apple fan, Colbert also once jokingly stated that he would love to play Steve Jobs. ("iPad, iPhone, iPod, iMac—he's the only person more obsessed with I than I am."[29]) On a more serious note, one of the few times Colbert has broken character on *The Colbert Report* was in his heartfelt tribute to Jobs after the computer mogul's 2011 death.

A certainty is a new Colbert book coming out in 2012, in time for the election excitement: *America Again: Re-Becoming the Greatness We Never Weren't.*

But most definitely, there will be *The Colbert Report*, ever a font of truthiness in a world of wikiality. There is not much Colbert does not like about the job he has landed in. "I love being onstage," he said. "I love the relationship with the audience. I love the letting go, the sense of discovery, the improvising."[30] In fact, Colbert jokingly refers to *The Colbert Report* as "The Joy Machine." The nickname comes from a piece of paper taped to the computer in his Manhattan office, which states, "'Joy is the most infallible sign of the presence of God.'" That joy animates what Stephen does, every day. "[I]f you can do [the show] with joy, even in the simplest show, then it's 'The Joy Machine' as opposed to 'The Machine.' Considering the speed at which we do it, we'll get caught in the gears really quickly unless we also approach it with joy."[31]

Neither does Colbert consider his show "a stepping stone. I really like what I'm doing." And he intends to keep doing it "as long as I can keep up the energy."[32] (He has joked that he will retire "thirty minutes after Jon Stewart does."[33]) Colbert "really believes he is changing the world one factual error at a time"[34] "by catching it in the headlights of [his] justice."[35]

It is quite a serious goal for a man who has built his life on comedy.

NOTES

1. Strauss, Neil. "The Subversive Joy of Stephen Colbert. (cover story)." *Rolling Stone* 1087 (2009): 56. MAS Ultra—School Edition. EBSCO. Web. 13 Oct. 2011.

2. Solomon, Deborah. "Funny About the News." *The New York Times Magazine*. 25 Sept. 2005: 18(L). *General OneFile*.

3. Peyser, Marc. "The Truthiness Teller; Stephen Colbert loves this country like he loves himself. Comedy Central's hot news anchor is a goofy caricature of our blustery culture. But he's starting to make sense." *Newsweek*. 13 Feb. 2006: 50. *General OneFile*. Web. 23 July 2010.

4. Mnookin, Seth. "The Man in the Irony Mask; Like Sacha Baron Cohen as Borat, Stephen Colbert so completely inhabits his creation— the arch-conservative blowhard host of The Colbert Report, his Daily Show spin-off hit—that he rarely breaks character." *Vanity Fair*. Oct. 2007: 342. *General OneFile*. Web. 23 July 2010.

5. Sternbergh, Adam. "Stephen Colbert has America by the ballots: the former Jon Stewart protégé created an entire comic persona out of right-wing doublespeak, trampling the boundary between parody and politics. Which makes him the perfect spokesman for a political season in which everything is imploding." *New York*. 16 Oct. 2006: 22+. *General OneFile*. Web. 23 July 2010.

6. Schorn, Daniel. "The Colbert Report—CBS News." *Breaking News Headlines: Business, Entertainment & World News—CBS News*. Web. 16 July 2010. <http://www.cbsnews.com/stories/2006/04/27/60minutes/main1553506.shtml>.

7. "Watch Colbert On Comedy Online—VideoSurf Video Search." *VideoSurf Video Search Engine | Watch Free Videos Online, Funny Videos, TV Episodes, Movies and More*. Web. 26 July 2011. <http://www.videosurf.com/video/colbert-on-comedy-12277896>.

8. Strauss, Neil. "Stephen Colbert on Deconstructing the News, Religion and the Colbert Nation | Culture News | Rolling Stone." *Rolling Stone | Music News, Politics, Reviews, Photos, Videos, Interviews and More*.

2 Sept. 2009. Web. 12 Oct. 2011. http://www.rollingstone.com/culture/news/stephen-colbert-on-deconstructing-the-news-religion-and-the-colbert-nation-20090902.

9. Solomon, Deborah. "Funny About the News." *The New York Times Magazine*. 25 Sept. 2005: 18(L). *General OneFile*.

10. Strauss, "Stephen Colbert on Deconstructing the News."

11. "How Did Stephen Break His Wrist?—The Colbert Report—2007-26-07—VideoClip | ComedyCentral."*ColbertNation | TheColbert Report | Comedy Central*. Web. 01 Aug. 2011. <http://www.colbertna tion.com/the-colbert-report-videos/90524/july-26-2007/how-did-ste phen-break-his-wrist->.

12. "Stephen Colbert, DonorsChoose.org, and the Gates Foundation: a News and Photo Recap." *No Fact Zone*. 23 Apr. 2009. Web. 01 Aug. 2011. <http://www.nofactzone.net/2009/04/23/stephen-colbert-donorschooseorg-and-the-gates-foundation-a-news-a>.

13. "Stephen Colbert's Charity Work, Events, and Causes." *Celebrity Charity News, Events, Organizations & Causes*. Web. 01 Aug. 2011. <http://www.looktothestars.org/celebrity/360-stephen-colbert>.

14. AlterNet. "Stephen Colbert's Address to the Graduates | Media | AlterNet." *Home | AlterNet*. Web. 01 Aug. 2011. <http://www.alternet.org/media/37144>.

15. "Stephen Colbert's Northwestern University Commencement Address. Transcript.—Lynn Sweet." *Chicago Sun-Times Blogs*. Web. 01 Aug. 2011. <http://blogs.suntimes.com/sweet/2011/06/stephen_col berts_northwestern_.html>

16. "Gorillaz—The Colbert Report—2010-22-04—Video Clip | ComedyCentral."*ColbertNation | TheColbertReport | ComedyCentral*. 22 Apr. 2010. Web. 12 Oct. 2011. <http://www.colbertnation.com/the-colbert-report-videos/281882/april-22-2010/gorillaz/>.

17. Sternbergh.

18. "Watch Colbert."

19. Peyser.

20. Mnookin.

21. Ferguson, D. B. "Stephen Colbert Accepts His 2007 Peabody Award." *No Fact Zone*. 16 June 2008. Web. 07 Aug. 2011. <http://www.nofactzone.net/2008/06/16/4254/>.

22. Ferguson, D. B. "Exclusive Interview: Rev. Sir Dr. Stephen T. Colbert, D.F.A." *No Fact Zone*. 17 May 2011. Web. 23 July 2011. <http://www.nofactzone.net/2011/05/21/exclusive-interview-rev-sir-dr-stephen-t-colbert-d-f-a/>.

23. Ferguson, "Exclusive Interview."

24. Edwards, Gavin. "Colbert Country." *Rolling Stone* 986 (2005): 68. MAS Ultra—School Edition. EBSCO. Web. 16 Oct. 2011.

25. Ferguson, "Exclusive Interview."

26. Peyser.

27. Edwards.

28. P., Ken. "IGN: An Interview with Stephen Colbert." *IGN Movies: Trailers, Movie Reviews, Pictures, Celebrities, and Interviews*. 11 Aug. 2003. Web. 12 Oct. 2011. <http://movies.ign.com/articles/433/433111 p1.html>.

29. "Stephen Colbert. (cover story)." *Entertainment Weekly* 1105/ 1106 (2010): 60. MAS Ultra—School Edition. EBSCO. Web. 16 Oct. 2011.

30. Mnookin.

31. Strauss, Neil. "The Subversive Joy of Stephen Colbert. (cover story)." *Rolling Stone* 1087 (2009): 56. MAS Ultra—School Edition. EBSCO. Web. 13 Oct. 2011.

32. "Charlie Rose—A Conversation with Comedian Stephen Colbert." *Charlie Rose—Home*. 8 Dec. 2006. Web. 23 Aug. 2011. <http://www.charlierose.com/view/interview/93>.

33. Kirschling, Gregory. "Stephen Colbert. (cover story)." *Entertainment Weekly* 941/942 (2007): 99. MAS Ultra—School Edition. EBSCO. Web. 16 Oct. 2011.

34. Peyser.

35. "Charlie Rose."

BIBLIOGRAPHY

AlterNet. "Stephen Colbert's Address to the Graduates | Media | AlterNet." *Home | AlterNet*. Web. 19 July 2011. <http://www.alternet.org/media/37144>.

Barlow, Rich. "One Class, One Day: Colbert 101 | BU Today." *Boston University*. 11 Mar. 2011. Web. 23 Aug. 2011. <http://www.bu.edu/today/node/12616>.

Baumgartner, Jody C., and Jonathan S. Morris. "One 'Nation,' Under Stephen? The Effects of The Colbert Report on American Youth." *Journal of Broadcasting & Electronic Media* 52.4 (2008): 622+. *General OneFile*. Web. 22 July 2010.

The Best of The Colbert Report. Comedy Central, 2007. DVD.

Bierly, Mandi. "The Colbert Report: How to Succeed in the TV Business by Really, Really Trying. Five Tips From Stephen Colbert on the Eve of His New Series." *Entertainment Weekly*. 21 Oct. 2005: 34. *General OneFile*. Web. 23 July 2010.

Boucher, Geoff. "Newsmakers; Colbert teams with Spider-Man; Stephen Colbert's presidential bid was never serious stuff in the real world, but in the pages of Marvel Comics, the Comedy

Central parodist's campaign is alive and well." *Houston Chronicle*. [Houston, TX] 1 Oct. 2008: 2. *General OneFile*. Web. 23 July 2010.

Brennan, Carol. "Colbert, Stephen (1964–)." *Newsmakers*. Vol. 4. Detroit: Gale, 2007. *Discovering Collection*. Web. 19 July 2011.

Brooks, Tim. "Current Bibliography." *ARSC Journal* 39.2 (2008): 357+. *Academic OneFile*. Web. 23 July 2010.

Carol, Memmott. "Colbert Reports on why he is a Great American." *USA Today*. n.d.: MAS Ultra—School Edition. EBSCO. Web. 16 Oct. 2011.

"Charlie Rose—A Conversation with Comedian Stephen Colbert." *Charlie Rose—Home*. 8 Dec. 2006. Web. 23 Aug. 2011. <http://www.charlierose.com/view/interview/93>.

Cheever, Benjamin. "Talking with Stephen Colbert. (Contemporary Culture) (Interview)." *AudioFile Magazine*. Oct.–Nov. 2007: 31. *General OneFile*. Web. 23 July 2010.

The Colbert Report. New York. 13 July 2011. Performance.

Colbert, Stephen. *I Am America (And So Can You!)*. New York: Grand Central Pub., 2007.

Colbert, Stephen T. "A Note From Stephen Colbert—Newsweek." *Newsweek—National News, World News, Business, Health, Technology, Entertainment, and More—Newsweek*. Web. 21 July 2011. <http://www.newsweek.com/2009/06/05/a-note-from-stephen-colbert.html>.

Colbert, Stephen T. "Why I Took This Crummy Job—Newsweek." *Newsweek—National News, World News, Business, Health, Technology, Entertainment, and More—Newsweek*. Web. 21 July 2011. <http://www.newsweek.com/2009/06/05/why-i-took-this-crummy-job.html>.

Dean, Josh. "Colbert on Ice." *Rolling Stone* 1098 (2010): 28. MAS Ultra—School Edition. EBSCO. Web. 16 Oct. 2011.

Dowd, Maureen. "America's Anchors (cover story)." *Rolling Stone* 1013 (2006): 52. MAS Ultra—School Edition. EBSCO. Web. 13 Oct. 2011.

"Dreamworks Returns with Star-Studded Cast of Voices." *Post-Standard*. [Syracuse, NY] 22 Mar. 2009: 18. *iCONN Custom Newspapers— U.S. Newspapers*. Web. 23 July 2010.

Edwards, Gavin. "Colbert Country." *Rolling Stone* 986 (2005): 68. MAS Ultra—School Edition. EBSCO. Web. 16 Oct. 2011.

Ferguson, D. B. "Exclusive Interview: Rev. Sir Dr. Stephen T. Colbert, D.F.A." *No Fact Zone.* 17 May 2011. Web. 23 July 2011. <http://www. nofactzone.net/2011/05/21/exclusive-interview-rev-sir-dr-stephen-t-colbert-d-f-a/>.

Ferguson, D. B. "Exclusive! Interview with Scott Chantler (Illustrator, 'Tek Jansen' Miniseries), Part 1." *No Fact Zone.* 1 Apr. 2007. Web. 21 Aug. 2011. <http://www.nofactzone.net/2007/04/01/exclusive-interview-with-scott-chantler-illustrator-tek-jansen-miniseries-part-1/>.

Ferguson, D. B. "Exclusive! Interview with Scott Chantler (Illustrator, 'Tek Jansen' Miniseries), Part 2." *No Fact Zone.* 3 Apr. 2007. Web. 21 Aug. 2011. <http://www.nofactzone.net/2007/04/03/exclusive-interview-with-scott-chantler-illustrator-tek-jansen-miniseries-part-2/>.

Ferguson, D. B. "Exclusive! Interview with Scott Chantler (Illustrator, 'Tek Jansen' Miniseries), Part 3." *No Fact Zone.* 5 Apr. 2007. Web. 21 Aug. 2011. <http://www.nofactzone.net/2007/04/05/exclu sive-interview-with-scott-chantler-illustrator-tek-jansen-mini series-part-3/>.

Ferguson, D. B. "Exclusive! Interview with Tom Peyer, 'Tek Jansen' Comic Author." *No Fact Zone.* 16 Feb. 2007. Web. 21 Aug. 2011. <http://www.nofactzone.net/2007/02/16/exclusive-interview-with-tom-peyer-tek-jansen-comic-author/>.

Ferguson, D. B. "Six Degrees: Interview with 'Colbert Christmas' Lyricist David Javerbaum." *No Fact Zone.* 1 Dec. 2008. Web. 21 Aug. 2011. <http://www.nofactzone.net/2008/12/01/six-degrees-interview-with-colbert-christmas-lyricist-david-javerbaum/>.

"First Show—The Colbert Report—2005-17-10—Video Clip | Comedy Central." *Colbert Nation | The Colbert Report | Comedy Central.* 17 Oct. 2005. Web. 28 Aug. 2011. <http://www.colbertnation. com/the-colbert-report-videos/180903/october-17-2005/>.

"Full List—Top 10 Stephen Colbert Moments—Time." *Breaking News, Analysis, Politics, Blogs, News Photos, Video, Tech Reviews—TIME. com.* Web. 21 July 2011. <http://www.time.com/time/specials/pack ages/completelist/0,29569,2027834,00.html>.

Gaiman, Neil. "Newbery Medal Acceptance." *The Horn Book Magazine* 85.4 (2009): 343+. *General OneFile*. Web. 23 July 2010.

Gancarski, A. G. "The Truthiness Shall Set You Free." *The American Conservative* 6.23 (2007): 33+. *Academic OneFile*. Web. 22 July 2010.

"Gorillaz—The Colbert Report—2010-22-04—Video Clip | Comedy Central." *Colbert Nation | The Colbert Report | Comedy Central.* 22 Apr. 2010. Web. 28 Aug. 2011. <http://www.colbertnation.com/the-colbert-report-videos/281882/april-22-2010/gorillaz>.

Gross, Terry. "Bluster and Satire: Stephen Colbert's 'Report': NPR." *NPR: National Public Radio: News & Analysis, World, US, Music & Arts: NPR.* 7 Dec. 2005. Web. 28 Aug. 2011. <http://www.npr.org/templates/story/story.php?storyid=5040948>.

Gross, Terry. "A Fake Newsman's Fake Newsman: Stephen Colbert: NPR." *NPR: National Public Radio: News & Analysis, World, US, Music & Arts: NPR.* 24 Jan. 2005. Web. 28 Aug. 2011. <http://www.npr.org/templates/story/story.php?storyid=4464017>.

Hamm, Theodore. *The New Blue Media: How Michael Moore, MoveOn. org, Jon Stewart and Company Are Transforming Progressive Politics.* New York: New Press, 2008. Print.

"Hearing of the Immigration, Citizenship, Refugees, Border Security, and International Law Subcommittee of the House Judiciary Committee Subject: Protecting America's Harvest Chaired by: Representative Zoe Lofgren (D-CA) Witnesses: Arturo Rodriguez, President, United Farm Workers; Phil Glaize, Chairman, U.S. Apple Association; Carol Swain, Professor, Vanderbilt University Law School; Stephen Colbert, . . ." *Congressional Hearing Transcript Database* 24 Sept. 2010. *General OneFile*. Web. 6 Mar. 2011.

Hymel, Kevin M. "Salute to Servicemembers: Comedian Stephen Colbert Inspires Troops at Home and Abroad." *Soldiers Magazine* 66.2 (2011): 16+. *General OneFile*. Web. 6 Mar. 2011.

"King of The Road." *The Hotline* (2010). *General OneFile*. Web. 22 July 2010.

Kurtz, Howard. "This Cracks Me Up." *Washingtonpost.com.* 23 Oct. 2007. *General OneFile*. Web. 23 July 2010.

"Laugh at Them All You Like, These Guys are Serious About Civility in Politics." *Australian*. [National, Australia] 23 Oct. 2010: 7. *Academic OneFile*. Web. 6 Mar. 2011.

Meacham, Jon. "A Reader's Guide to the Colbert Issue." *Newsweek* 153.24 (2009): 2. MAS Ultra—School Edition. EBSCO. Web. 16 Oct. 2011.

"Measuring the 'Colbert Bump': Do Politicians Raise More Funds After Appearing on The Colbert Report Comedy Show?" *US Newswire*. 13 Aug. 2008. *General OneFile*. Web. 28 July 2011.

Michaels, Wendy. "Stephen Colbert." *Celebrity Gossip, Oops and News*. Web. 9 July 2011. http://celebrity.lovetoknow.com/Stephen_Colbert.

Mimms, Sarah. "FEC Rules Narrowly on Colbert Request." *National journal.com*. 30 June 2011. *General OneFile*. Web. 19 July 2011.

Mitchell, Greg. "Obama Owes It All To—Stephen Colbert!" *Editor & Publisher*. (2008). *General OneFile*. Web. 28 July 2011.

Mitchell, Greg. "Two Years Ago: When Stephen Colbert Mocked the President—and the Media—After Dinner." *Editor & Publisher* (2008). *General OneFile*. Web. 11 July 2011.

Mnookin, Seth. "The Man in the Irony Mask; Like Sacha Baron Cohen as Borat, Stephen Colbert so completely inhabits his creation-the arch-conservative blowhard host of The Colbert Report, his Daily Show spin-off hit-that he rarely breaks character." *Vanity Fair*. Oct. 2007: 342. *General OneFile*. Web. 23 July 2010.

"NASA Treadmill Named for Stephen Colbert; Comedian and talk show host gets a consolation prize for his effort to have an International Space Station node named after him." *InformationWeek*. (2009). *General OneFile*. Web. 23 July 2010.

"NBC's Today Show, 8:00 am." *Today*. [Transcript] 19 Mar. 2009. *General OneFile*. Web. 23 July 2010.

"News Filter: Navigating the New Media." *The Christian Century* 126.19 (2009): 22+. *General OneFile*. Web. 23 July 2010.

P., Ken. "IGN: An Interview with Stephen Colbert." *IGN Movies: Trailers, Movie Reviews, Pictures, Celebrities, and Interviews*. 11 Aug. 2003. Web. 12 Oct. 2011. <http://movies.ign.com/articles/433/433111p1.html>.

P., Ken. "IGN: 10 Questions: Stephen Colbert." *IGN Movies: Trailers, Movie Reviews, Pictures, Celebrities, and Interviews.* 25 June 2003. Web. 12 Oct. 2011. <http://movies.ign.com/articles/425/425845p1.html>.

Peyser, Marc. "The Truthiness Teller; Stephen Colbert loves this country like he loves himself. Comedy Central's hot news anchor is a goofy caricature of our blustery culture. But he's starting to make sense." *Newsweek.* 13 Feb. 2006: 50. *General OneFile.* Web. 23 July 2010.

Phillips, Jennifer. "Humour, Political Satire, and Ironic Tension Between the 'Real' and the 'Fictional' Stephen Colbert." Thesis. University of Wollogong, 2010. Web. 20 Aug. 2011. <http://www.polsis.uq.edu.au/docs/Challenging-Politics-Papers/Jennifer_Phillips_Humour_Political_Satire_and_Ironic_Tension.pdf>.

Plys, Cate. "The Real Stephen Colbert: Northwestern Magazine—Northwestern University." *Home: Northwestern University.* Web. 10 December 2010. <http://www.northwestern.edu/magazine/winter2010/feature/the-real-stephen-colbert.html>.

Poniewozik, James. "The American Bald Ego: Leaving his perch at The Daily Show, Stephen Colbert is soaring to new heights of media parody." *Time.* 14 Nov. 2005: 68. *General OneFile.* Web. 23 July 2010.

Poniewozik, James. "Can These Guys Be Serious?" *Time* 176.18 (2010): 91. MAS Ultra—School Edition. EBSCO. Web. 14 Oct. 2011.

Rabin, Nathan. "Interview with Stephen Colbert from The Onion's AV Club." *Enter Tony's "Strangers With Candy Companion."* 26 Jan. 2006. Web. 31 July 2011. <http://www.jerriblank.com/colbert_onion-av-club.html>.

Read, Brock. "Building an Encyclopedia, With or Without Scholars." *The Chronicle of Higher Education* 53.10 (2006). *General OneFile.* Web. 23 July 2010.

"The Real Stephen Colbert (Out of Character)—YouTube." *YouTube—Broadcast Yourself.* Web. 23 July 2011. <http://www.youtube.com/watch?v=DNvJZCFpdp8>.

Remnick, David. "Reporter Guy." *The New Yorker.* 25 July 2005: 38. *General OneFile.* Web. 11 July 2011.

Robertson, Campbell. "Stephen Colbert Takes His Show on the Road to Baghdad—NYTimes.com." *The New York Times—Breaking News,*

World News & Multimedia. 18 July 2011. Web. 18 July 2011. <http://www.nytimes.com/2009/06/08/arts/television/08colb. html>.

Robson, David. ". . . and one you use to design a president." *New Scientist* 198.2652 (2008): 22. *Academic OneFile.* Web. 23 July 2010.

Rogak, Lisa. *And Nothing but the Truthiness: the Rise (and Further Rise) of Stephen Colbert.* New York: Thomas Dunne, 2011. Print.

Schiller, Aaron Allen. *Stephen Colbert and Philosophy: I Am Philosophy (and so Can You!).* Chicago, IL: Open Court, 2009. Print.

Schneider, Craig. "D.C. Rally Draws Crowds, Laughs: Comedians Keep Event Light—With Some Political Undertones. Stewart said goal was also to provide hope." *Atlanta Journal-Constitution* [Atlanta, GA] 31 Oct. 2010: A2. *General OneFile.* Web. 6 Mar. 2011.

Schorn, Daniel. "The Colbert Report—CBS News." *Breaking News Headlines: Business, Entertainment & World News—CBS News.* Web. 16 July 2010. <http://www.cbsnews.com/stories/2006/04/ 27/60minutes/main1553506.shtml>.

"Scoop: Stephen Colbert Gets New Ben & Jerry's Ice Cream Flavor." *Editor & Publisher.* (2007). *General OneFile.* Web. 23 July 2010.

Seitz, Jonathan. "It's an Online World for Young People and Political News." *Nieman Reports* 62.2 (2008): 10+. *General OneFile.* Web. 23 July 2010.

Solomon, Deborah. "Funny About the News." *The New York Times Magazine.* 25 Sept. 2005: 18(L). *General OneFile.*

Staff, E and P. "Stephen Colbert Appears on 'Meet the Press' to Discuss Race for President." *Editor & Publisher.* (2007). *General OneFile.* Web. 23 July 2010.

Starnes, Bobby Ann. "On Truthiness, Wiki-ality, and Driving on a Treadmill." *Phi Delta Kappan* 88.2 (2006): 173. *General OneFile.* Web. 22 July 2010.

"Stephen Colbert." *Contemporary Authors Online.* Detroit: Gale, 2009. *Literature Resource Center.* Web. 21 Aug. 2011.

"Stephen Colbert Cops to Killing Mr. Goodwrench." *Jalopnik—Drive Free or Die.* Web. 18 July 2011. <http://jalopnik.com/5691385/stephen-colbert-cops-to-killing-mr-goodwrench>.

"Stephen Colbert: I Am America and So Can You." *iTunes: Meet the Author.* 27 Oct. 2007. Web. 28 Aug. 2011. <http://itunes.apple.com/us/podcast/itunes-meet-the-author/id=266215977>.

"Stephen Colbert—IMDb." *The Internet Movie Database (IMDb).* Web. 19 July 2011. <http://www.imdb.com/name/nm0170306/>.

"Stephen Colbert: In Good 'Company' On Broadway." *Fresh Air.* 14 June 2011. *General OneFile.* Web. 19 July 2011.

"Stephen Colbert Sings in Sondheim Show." *The Post and Courier, Charleston SC—News, Sports, Entertainment.* 24 Apr. 2011. Web. 24 July 2011. <http://www.postandcourier.com/news/2011/apr/24/colbert-sings-in-sondheim-show/>.

"Stephen Colbert's Northwestern University Commencement Address. Transcript.—Lynn Sweet." *Chicago Sun-Times Blogs.* Web. 19 July 2011. <http://blogs.suntimes.com/sweet/2011/06/stephen_colbe rts_northwestern_.html>.

Sternbergh, Adam. "Stephen Colbert has America by the ballots: the former Jon Stewart Protégé created an entire comic persona out of right-wing doublespeak, trampling the boundary between parody and politics. Which makes him the perfect spokesman for a political season in which everything is imploding." *New York.* 16 Oct. 2006: 22+. *General OneFile.* Web. 23 July 2010.

"Stewart-Colbert Rally Pegged at 215,000." *Canadian Broadcasting Corporation* [CBC]. 1 Nov. 2010. *General OneFile.* Web. 19 July 2011.

Strauss, Neil. "Stephen Colbert on Deconstructing the News, Religion and the Colbert Nation | Culture News | Rolling Stone." *Rolling Stone | Music News, Politics, Reviews, Photos, Videos, Interviews and More.* 2 Sept. 2009. Web. 12 Oct. 2011. <http://www.rollingstone.com/culture/news/stephen-colbert-on-deconstructing-the-news-religion-and-the-colbert-nation-20090902>.

Strauss, Neil. "The Subversive Joy of Stephen Colbert. (cover story)." *Rolling Stone* 1087 (2009): 56. MAS Ultra—School Edition. EBSCO. Web. 13 Oct. 2011.

Streuli, Stuart. "Stephen Colbert Challenges You to an Ocean Race." *Sailing World.* May 2011: 30+. *General OneFile.* Web. 12 Oct. 2011.

SW. "Reviews: Stephen & Evelyn Colbert Perform 'Old Times' at Luna Stage Benefit." *No Fact Zone.* 13 Jan. 2011. Web. 16 Oct. 2011.

<http://www.nofactzone.net/2011/01/13/reviews-stephen-evelyn-colbert-perform-old-times-at-luna-stage-benefit/>.

Tavernise, Sabrina, and Brian Stelter. "At Washington Rally by Two Satirists, Thousands—Billions?—Respond." *New York Times.* 31 Oct. 2010: A24(L). *General OneFile.* Web. 6 Mar. 2011.

"Tek Jansen Theme Song." *PoeTV.* Web. 21 Aug. 2011. <http://www.poetv.com/video.php?vid=11587>.

"'Truthiness' picked as word of the year." *The Quill* 95.1 (2007): 5. *General OneFile.* Web. 23 July 2010.

"U. South Carolina Students Discuss Colbert's Presidential Bid." *Daily Gamecock* [Columbia, SC]. 19 Oct. 2007. *iCONN Custom Newspapers—U.S. Newspapers.* Web. 23 July 2010.

Vance, Erik. "Race for Survival." *The Chronicle of Higher Education* 53.37 (2007). *General OneFile.* Web. 23 July 2010.

"Watch Colbert On Comedy Online—VideoSurf Video Search." *VideoSurf Video Search Engine | Watch Free Videos Online, Funny Videos, TV Episodes, Movies and More.* Web. 26 July 2011. <http://www.videosurf.com/video/colbert-on-comedy-12277896>.

Weinman, Jaime J. "The Secret Agenda of Stephen Colbert: In Two Years, He's Turned a 'Daily Show' Spinoff into a Wacky Sitcom." *Maclean's.* 22 Oct. 2007: 57+. *General OneFile.* Web. 23 July 2010.

"White House Correspondents' Dinner Stephen Colbert Transcript." *Political Humor—Jokes Satire and Political Cartoons.* Web. 9 July 2011. http://politicalhumor.about.com/od/stephencolbert/a/colbertbush_2.htm?p=1.

Winston, Kimberly. "Quiet Faith Lies Behind Satirist's Blowhard Facade." *The Christian Century* 127.23 (2010): 16. *General OneFile.* Web. 6 Mar. 2011.

Wolk, Josh. "Mock the Vote." *Entertainment Weekly.* 3 Oct. 2008: 34. *General OneFile.* Web. 23 July 2010.

Wood, James. "MSM S&M." *New Republic* 234.19 (2006): 42. MAS Ultra—School Edition. EBSCO. Web. 16 Oct. 2011.

INDEX

About the Author

CATHERINE M. ANDRONIK, besides writing biographies for children and young adults, has been a school librarian for more than 25 years. Currently, she works in that position at Brien McMahon High School in Norwalk, Connecticut. She is an avid traveler, which gives her lots of time to indulge in her other favorite pastime, reading. A graduate of Wesleyan University in Middletown, Connecticut, with a B.A. in English, she is currently enrolled in a mostly online Ph.D. program at Charles Sturt University in Bathurst, Australia, where she is researching fiction for young adults by authors from Down Under.